2017 SQA Specimen and Past Papers with Answers

National 5
PHYSICS

2015 & 2017 Exams
and 2017 Specimen Question Paper

Hodder Gibson Study Skills Advice – National 5 Physics	– page 3
Hodder Gibson Study Skills Advice – General	– page 5
2015 EXAM	– page 7
2017 EXAM	– page 55
2017 SPECIMEN QUESTION PAPER	– page 107
ANSWERS	– page 161

HODDER GIBSON
AN HACHETTE UK COMPANY

This book contains the official SQA 2015 and 2017 Exams, and the 2017 Specimen Question Paper for National 5 Physics, with associated SQA-approved answers modified from the official marking instructions that accompany the paper.

In addition the book contains study skills advice. This advice has been specially commissioned by Hodder Gibson, and has been written by experienced senior teachers and examiners in line with the new National 5 syllabus. This is not SQA material but has been devised to provide further guidance for National 5 examinations.

Hodder Gibson is grateful to the copyright holders, as credited on the final page of the Answer section, for permission to use their material. Every effort has been made to trace the copyright holders and to obtain their permission for the use of copyright material. Hodder Gibson will be happy to receive information allowing us to rectify any error or omission in future editions.

Hachette UK's policy is to use papers that are natural, renewable and recyclable products and made from wood grown in sustainable forests. The logging and manufacturing processes are expected to conform to the environmental regulations of the country of origin.

Orders: please contact Bookpoint Ltd, 130 Park Drive, Milton Park, Abingdon, Oxon OX14 4SE. Telephone: (44) 01235 827720. Fax: (44) 01235 400454. Lines are open 9.00–5.00, Monday to Saturday, with a 24-hour message answering service. Visit our website at www.hoddereducation.co.uk. Hodder Gibson can be contacted direct on: Tel: 0141 333 4650; Fax: 0141 404 8188; email: hoddergibson@hodder.co.uk

This collection first published in 2017 by
Hodder Gibson, an imprint of Hodder Education,
An Hachette UK Company
211 St Vincent Street
Glasgow G2 5QY

National 5 2015 and 2017 Exam Papers and Answers; 2017 Specimen Question Paper and Answers © Scottish Qualifications Authority. Study Skills section © Hodder Gibson. All rights reserved. Apart from any use permitted under UK copyright law, no part of this publication may be reproduced or transmitted in any form or by any means, electronic or mechanical, including photocopying and recording, or held within any information storage and retrieval system, without permission in writing from the publisher or under licence from the Copyright Licensing Agency Limited. Further details of such licences (for reprographic reproduction) may be obtained from the Copyright Licensing Agency Limited, www.cla.co.uk

Typeset by Aptara, Inc.

Printed in the UK

A catalogue record for this title is available from the British Library

ISBN: 978-1-5104-2198-1

2 1

2018 2017

Introduction

National 5 Physics

This book of SQA past papers contains the question papers used in the 2015* and 2017 exams (with the answers at the back of the book). The National 5 Physics exam is being extended by 20 marks from 2018 onwards, following the removal of unit assessments from the course. A new specimen question paper, which reflects the requirements of the extended exam, is also included. The specimen question paper reflects the content and duration of the exam in 2018. All of the question papers included in the book (2015, 2017 and the new specimen question paper) provide excellent practice for the final exams.

Using the 2015 and 2017 past papers as part of your revision will help you to develop the vital skills and techniques needed for the exam, and will help you to identify any knowledge gaps you may have.

* Questions from the 2016 past paper have been used to create the new specimen question paper. To avoid duplication and provide you with optimum variety of questions, we have intentionally included the 2015 past paper instead.

The exam

Duration: 2 ½ hours
Total marks: 135

25 marks are awarded for 25 **multiple-choice questions** – completed on an answer grid.

110 marks are awarded for **written answers** – completed in the space provided after each question or on graph paper.

The National 5 Physics course includes the following areas of physics:

- Dynamics
- Space
- Electricity
- Properties of matter
- Waves
- Radiation

The 135 marks are made up of questions taken from these areas of physics.

General exam advice

There are 135 marks in total, and you have two and a half hours to complete the paper. This works out at just over one minute per mark, so a 10-mark question would take roughly 11 minutes.

Be aware of how much time you spend on each question. For example, DO NOT spend 10 minutes on a question worth only 3 marks, especially when you haven't completed the rest of the questions – you can always return to the question later if there's time.

The best method for getting used to National 5 exam questions is to attempt as many exam type questions as possible, **and check your answers**. If you find a wrong answer, **find out why it is wrong** and then try similar questions until you can answer them correctly.

Specific exam advice

Advice for answering multiple-choice questions (Section 1) (25 marks)

Each question has five possible choices of answers. **Only one answer is correct.**

Multiple-choice questions are designed to test a range of skills, e.g.

- knowledge and understanding of the course
- using equations
- selecting correct statements from a list
- selecting and analysing information from a diagram.

It is important to **practise** as many **multiple-choice questions** as possible, to get used to the "style" and types of questions.

Do not try to work out all of the answers to multiple-choice questions in your head. Instead, when the question is complicated, write down notes and work on scrap paper (provided by the invigilator) or use the blank pages at the end of the question paper.

Do not use the answer grid for working, and remember to cross out your multiple-choice rough working when you have finished.

You can also make notes beside the actual question, if this helps, but **not** on the answer grid.

Advice for answering written questions (Section 2) (110 marks)

These questions test several different skills.

The majority of these marks test your **knowledge and understanding** of the course.

There are also questions which test different skills, like selecting information, analysing information, predicting results, and commenting on experimental results.

There are usually around 12–16 questions in Section 2. There are different types of questions, which include:

- Questions testing your **knowledge of the course**, sometimes applied to particular applications. More than half of the 110 marks in Section 2 are for this type of question.

- Questions (usually a maximum of two) involving **physics content not in the course** but explained in the question. A new equation is usually given in this question, which you may be asked to use with given data to calculate an answer.
- A question testing your **scientific reading skills**, where you will be asked about a scientific report or passage. The question might include a calculation.
- **"Open-ended" questions** (a maximum of two per exam, 3 marks each), which usually discuss a physics phenomenon and ask you to explain it using your knowledge of physics. You have to think about the issue and try to give a step-by-step answer – there may be more than one area of physics required to answer this type of question. These questions allow you to use your knowledge and problem-solving skills. Be careful not to spend longer than necessary on these 3-mark questions.
- Questions testing practical skills usually based on **practical or experimental results**, which may consist of tables of results or graphs (or both) which have to be used to obtain information needed to answer the question. You could be asked to identify a problem with the results, or to suggest an improvement to the experiment.

Things to remember when answering questions

Using equations

More than half of the total marks awarded in Section 2 are for being able to calculate answers using an equation (relationship) from the **"Relationship Sheet"** which is supplied with the exam paper.

These questions are usually worth 3 marks. To obtain the full 3 marks for these questions, your final answer must be correct.

There are 3 separate marks awarded for the stages of the working:

- Write down the correct equation needed to calculate the answer from the Relationship Sheet – **1 mark**.
- Show that the correct values are substituted into the equation – **1 mark**.
- Show the final answer, including the correct unit – **1 mark**.

If the unit is wrong or missing, you will lose the final mark!

Other important areas to remember and practise are:

Units

The units of measurement in the National 5 Physics course are based on the International System of Units. Make sure that you use the correct unit following a calculation in your final answer.

Prefixes

A prefix produces a multiple of the unit in powers of ten, e.g. 10^{-6} is 0·000001. It is named "micro" and has the symbol "µ". Make sure to practise and get used to all prefixes.

Scientific notation

This is used in the exam to write very large or very small numbers, to avoid writing or using strings of numbers in an answer or calculation.

You need to be familiar with how to enter and use numbers in scientific notation using **your own** calculator – make sure that you have used your calculator often before the exam to get used to it.

Significant figures

When calculating a value using an equation, take care not to give too many significant figures in the final answer. If there are intermediate steps in a calculation, you can keep numbers in your calculator which have too many significant figures. You should always round your answer to give no more than the smallest number of significant figures which appear in the data given in the question.

E.g. $\frac{42 \cdot 74}{2 \cdot 59} = 16 \cdot 5019305$

If the smallest number of significant figures relating to the data used from the question was 3, then round this answer to 16·5.

Examples:

- 20 has 1 significant figure
- 40·0 has 3 significant figures
- 0·000604 has 3 significant figures
- $4 \cdot 30 \times 10^4$ has 3 significant figures
- 6200 has 2 significant figures

Good luck!

Remember that the rewards for passing National 5 Physics are well worth it! Your pass will help you get the future you want for yourself. In the exam, be confident in your own ability. If you are not sure how to answer a question, trust your instincts and just give it a go anyway. Keep calm and don't panic! GOOD LUCK!

Study Skills – what you need to know to pass exams!

Pause for thought

Many students might skip quickly through a page like this. After all, we all know how to revise. Do you really though?

Think about this:

"IF YOU ALWAYS DO WHAT YOU ALWAYS DO, YOU WILL ALWAYS GET WHAT YOU HAVE ALWAYS GOT."

Do you like the grades you get? Do you want to do better? If you get full marks in your assessment, then that's great! Change nothing! This section is just to help you get that little bit better than you already are.

There are two main parts to the advice on offer here. The first part highlights fairly obvious things but which are also very important. The second part makes suggestions about revision that you might not have thought about but which WILL help you.

Part 1

DOH! It's so obvious but …

Start revising in good time

Don't leave it until the last minute – this will make you panic.

Make a revision timetable that sets out work time AND play time.

Sleep and eat!

Obvious really, and very helpful. Avoid arguments or stressful things too – even games that wind you up. You need to be fit, awake and focused!

Know your place!

Make sure you know exactly **WHEN and WHERE** your exams are.

Know your enemy!

Make sure you know what to expect in the exam.

How is the paper structured?

How much time is there for each question?

What types of question are involved?

Which topics seem to come up time and time again?

Which topics are your strongest and which are your weakest?

Are all topics compulsory or are there choices?

Learn by DOING!

There is no substitute for past papers and practice papers – they are simply essential! Tackling this collection of papers and answers is exactly the right thing to be doing as your exams approach.

Part 2

People learn in different ways. Some like low light, some bright. Some like early morning, some like evening / night. Some prefer warm, some prefer cold. But everyone uses their BRAIN and the brain works when it is active. Passive learning – sitting gazing at notes – is the most INEFFICIENT way to learn anything. Below you will find tips and ideas for making your revision more effective and maybe even more enjoyable. What follows gets your brain active, and active learning works!

Activity 1 – Stop and review

Step 1

When you have done no more than 5 minutes of revision reading STOP!

Step 2

Write a heading in your own words which sums up the topic you have been revising.

Step 3

Write a summary of what you have revised in no more than two sentences. Don't fool yourself by saying, "I know it, but I cannot put it into words". That just means you don't know it well enough. If you cannot write your summary, revise that section again, knowing that you must write a summary at the end of it. Many of you will have notebooks full of blue/black ink writing. Many of the pages will not be especially attractive or memorable so try to liven them up a bit with colour as you are reviewing and rewriting. **This is a great memory aid, and memory is the most important thing.**

Activity 2 – Use technology!

Why should everything be written down? Have you thought about "mental" maps, diagrams, cartoons and colour to help you learn? And rather than write down notes, why not record your revision material?

What about having a text message revision session with friends? Keep in touch with them to find out how and what they are revising and share ideas and questions.

Why not make a video diary where you tell the camera what you are doing, what you think you have learned and what you still have to do? No one has to see or hear it, but the process of having to organise your thoughts in a formal way to explain something is a very important learning practice.

Be sure to make use of electronic files. You could begin to summarise your class notes. Your typing might be slow, but it will get faster and the typed notes will be easier to read than the scribbles in your class notes. Try to add different fonts and colours to make your work stand out. You can easily Google relevant pictures, cartoons and diagrams which you can copy and paste to make your work more attractive and **MEMORABLE**.

Activity 3 – This is it. Do this and you will know lots!

Step 1

In this task you must be very honest with yourself! Find the SQA National 5 Physics Course Specification for the 2017–2018 session onwards (www.sqa.org.uk). Look at how the Course Specification provides detailed information about the course. It describes the structure of the course in terms of the skills, knowledge and understanding that are assessed. That means stuff you MUST know.

Step 2

BEFORE you do ANY revision on this topic, write a list of everything that you already know about the subject. It might be quite a long list but you only need to write it once. It shows you all the information that is already in your long-term memory so you know what parts you do not need to revise!

Step 3

Pick a chapter or section from your book or revision notes. Choose a fairly large section or a whole chapter to get the most out of this activity.

With a buddy, use Skype, Facetime, Twitter or any other communication you have, to play the game "If this is the answer, what is the question?". For example, if you are revising Geography and the answer you provide is "meander", your buddy would have to make up a question like "What is the word that describes a feature of a river where it flows slowly and bends often from side to side?".

Make up 10 "answers" based on the content of the chapter or section you are using. Give this to your buddy to solve while you solve theirs.

Step 4

Construct a wordsearch of at least 10 × 10 squares. You can make it as big as you like but keep it realistic. Work together with a group of friends. Many apps allow you to make wordsearch puzzles online. The words and phrases can go in any direction and phrases can be split. Your puzzle must only contain facts linked to the topic you are revising. Your task is to find 10 bits of information to hide in your puzzle, but you must not repeat information that you used in Step 3. DO NOT show where the words are. Fill up empty squares with random letters. Remember to keep a note of where your answers are hidden but do not show your friends. When you have a complete puzzle, exchange it with a friend to solve each other's puzzle.

Step 5

Now make up 10 questions (not "answers" this time) based on the same chapter used in the previous two tasks. Again, you must find NEW information that you have not yet used. Now it's getting hard to find that new information! Again, give your questions to a friend to answer.

Step 6

As you have been doing the puzzles, your brain has been actively searching for new information. Now write a NEW LIST that contains only the new information you have discovered when doing the puzzles. Your new list is the one to look at repeatedly for short bursts over the next few days. Try to remember more and more of it without looking at it. After a few days, you should be able to add words from your second list to your first list as you increase the information in your long-term memory.

FINALLY! Be inspired...

Make a list of different revision ideas and beside each one write **THINGS I HAVE** tried, **THINGS I WILL** try and **THINGS I MIGHT** try. Don't be scared of trying something new.

And remember – "FAIL TO PREPARE AND PREPARE TO FAIL!"

NATIONAL 5
2015

N5 National Qualifications 2015

X757/75/02

Physics
Section 1—Questions

TUESDAY, 5 MAY
9:00 AM – 11:00 AM

Instructions for the completion of Section 1 are given on *Page two* of your question and answer booklet X757/75/01.

Record your answers on the answer grid on *Page three* of your question and answer booklet.

Reference may be made to the Data Sheet on *Page two* of this booklet and to the Relationship Sheet X757/75/11.

Before leaving the examination room you must give your question and answer booklet to the Invigilator; if you do not, you may lose all the marks for this paper.

SQA

DATA SHEET

Speed of light in materials

Material	Speed in m s^{-1}
Air	3.0×10^8
Carbon dioxide	3.0×10^8
Diamond	1.2×10^8
Glass	2.0×10^8
Glycerol	2.1×10^8
Water	2.3×10^8

Gravitational field strengths

	Gravitational field strength on the surface in N kg^{-1}
Earth	9.8
Jupiter	23
Mars	3.7
Mercury	3.7
Moon	1.6
Neptune	11
Saturn	9.0
Sun	270
Uranus	8.7
Venus	8.9

Specific latent heat of fusion of materials

Material	Specific latent heat of fusion in J kg^{-1}
Alcohol	0.99×10^5
Aluminium	3.95×10^5
Carbon Dioxide	1.80×10^5
Copper	2.05×10^5
Iron	2.67×10^5
Lead	0.25×10^5
Water	3.34×10^5

Specific latent heat of vaporisation of materials

Material	Specific latent heat of vaporisation in J kg^{-1}
Alcohol	11.2×10^5
Carbon Dioxide	3.77×10^5
Glycerol	8.30×10^5
Turpentine	2.90×10^5
Water	22.6×10^5

Speed of sound in materials

Material	Speed in m s^{-1}
Aluminium	5200
Air	340
Bone	4100
Carbon dioxide	270
Glycerol	1900
Muscle	1600
Steel	5200
Tissue	1500
Water	1500

Specific heat capacity of materials

Material	Specific heat capacity in J kg^{-1} °C^{-1}
Alcohol	2350
Aluminium	902
Copper	386
Glass	500
Ice	2100
Iron	480
Lead	128
Oil	2130
Water	4180

Melting and boiling points of materials

Material	Melting point in °C	Boiling point in °C
Alcohol	−98	65
Aluminium	660	2470
Copper	1077	2567
Glycerol	18	290
Lead	328	1737
Iron	1537	2737

Radiation weighting factors

Type of radiation	Radiation weighting factor
alpha	20
beta	1
fast neutrons	10
gamma	1
slow neutrons	3
X-rays	1

SECTION 1

Attempt ALL questions

1. Two circuits are set up as shown.

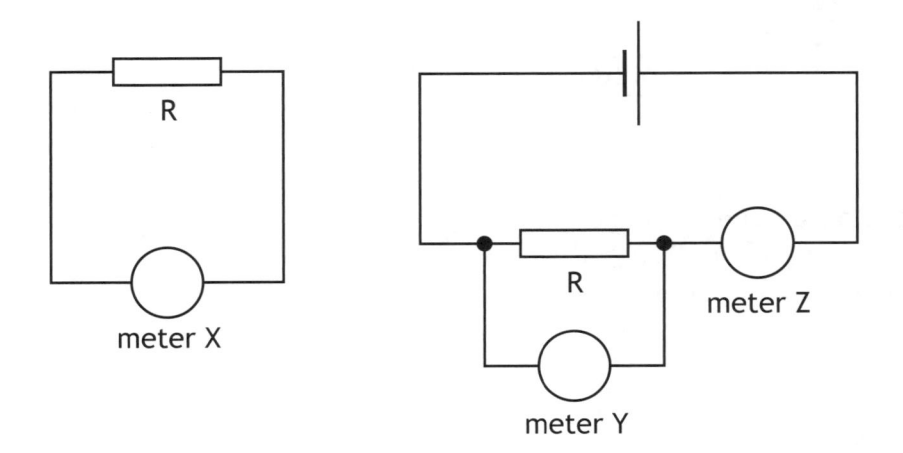

   Both circuits are used to determine the resistance of resistor R.

   Which row in the table identifies meter X, meter Y and meter Z?

	meter X	meter Y	meter Z
A	ohmmeter	voltmeter	ammeter
B	ohmmeter	ammeter	voltmeter
C	voltmeter	ammeter	ohmmeter
D	ammeter	voltmeter	ohmmeter
E	voltmeter	ohmmeter	ammeter

2. Which of the following statements is/are correct?

   I   The voltage of a battery is the number of joules of energy it gives to each coulomb of charge.

   II A battery only has a voltage when it is connected in a complete circuit.

   III Electrons are free to move within an insulator.

   A I only
   B II only
   C III only
   D II and III only
   E I, II and III

[Turn over

3. A circuit is set up as shown.

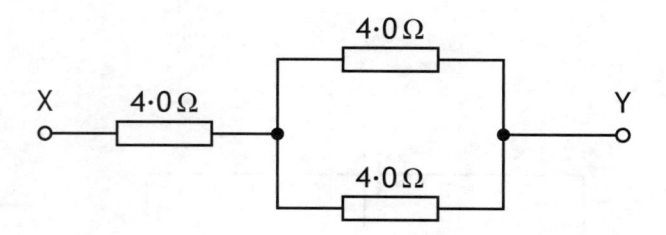

   The resistance between X and Y is

   A   1·3 Ω
   B   4·5 Ω
   C   6·0 Ω
   D   8·0 Ω
   E   12 Ω.

4. The rating plate on an electrical appliance is shown.

   230 V~
   50 Hz
   920 W
   model: HD 1055

   The resistance of this appliance is

   A   0·017 Ω
   B   0·25 Ω
   C   4·0 Ω
   D   18·4 Ω
   E   57·5 Ω.

5. A syringe containing air is sealed at one end as shown.

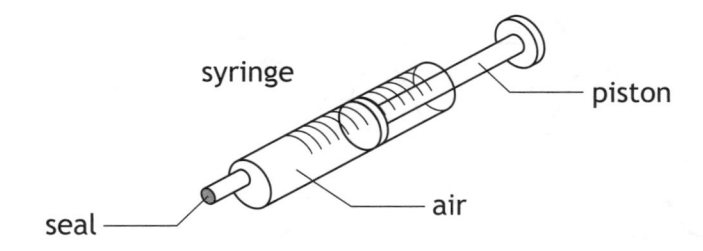

The piston is pushed in slowly.

There is no change in temperature of the air inside the syringe.

Which of the following statements describes and explains the change in pressure of the air in the syringe?

A   The pressure increases because the air particles have more kinetic energy.

B   The pressure increases because the air particles hit the sides of the syringe more frequently.

C   The pressure increases because the air particles hit the sides of the syringe less frequently.

D   The pressure decreases because the air particles hit the sides of the syringe with less force.

E   The pressure decreases because the air particles have less kinetic energy.

6. The pressure of a fixed mass of gas is 150 kPa at a temperature of 27 °C.

The temperature of the gas is now increased to 47 °C.

The volume of the gas remains constant.

The pressure of the gas is now

A   86 kPa
B   141 kPa
C   150 kPa
D   160 kPa
E   261 kPa.

[Turn over

Page five

7. The diagram represents a water wave.

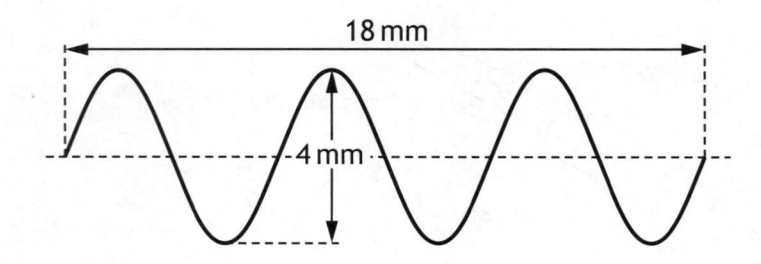

   The wavelength of the water wave is

   A   2 mm
   B   3 mm
   C   4 mm
   D   6 mm
   E   18 mm.

8. A student makes the following statements about different types of electromagnetic waves.

   I   Light waves are transverse waves.
   II Radio waves travel at 340 m s^{-1} through air.
   III Ultraviolet waves have a longer wavelength than infrared waves.

   Which of these statements is/are correct?

   A   I only
   B   I and II only
   C   I and III only
   D   II and III only
   E   I, II and III

9. Alpha radiation ionises an atom.

   Which statement describes what happens to the atom?

   A   The atom splits in half.
   B   The atom releases a neutron.
   C   The atom becomes positively charged.
   D   The atom gives out gamma radiation.
   E   The atom releases heat.

10. A sample of tissue is irradiated using a radioactive source.

    A student makes the following statements.

    The equivalent dose received by the tissue is

    I   reduced by shielding the tissue with a lead screen
    II increased as the distance from the source to the tissue is increased
    III increased by increasing the time of exposure of the tissue to the radiation.

    Which of the statements is/are correct?

    A   I only
    B   II only
    C   I and II only
    D   II and III only
    E   I and III only

11. A sample of tissue receives an absorbed dose of 16 µGy from alpha particles.

    The radiation weighting factor for alpha particles is 20.

    The equivalent dose received by the sample is

    A   0·80 µSv
    B   1·25 µSv
    C   4 µSv
    D   36 µSv
    E   320 µSv.

12. For a particular radioactive source, 240 atoms decay in 1 minute.

    The activity of this source is

    A   4 Bq
    B   180 Bq
    C   240 Bq
    D   300 Bq
    E   14 400 Bq.

[Turn over

13. The letters X, Y and Z represent missing words from the following passage.

    During a nuclear ……X…… reaction two nuclei of smaller mass number combine to produce a nucleus of larger mass number. During a nuclear ……Y…… reaction a nucleus of larger mass number splits into two nuclei of smaller mass number. Both of these reactions are important because these processes can release ……Z…… .

    Which row in the table shows the missing words?

	X	Y	Z
A	fusion	fission	electrons
B	fission	fusion	energy
C	fusion	fission	protons
D	fission	fusion	protons
E	fusion	fission	energy

14. Which of the following quantities is fully described by its magnitude?

    A   Force

    B   Displacement

    C   Energy

    D   Velocity

    E   Acceleration

15. The table shows the velocities of three objects X, Y and Z over a period of 3 seconds. Each object is moving in a straight line.

Time (s)	0	1	2	3
Velocity of X (m s^{-1})	2	4	6	8
Velocity of Y (m s^{-1})	0	1	2	3
Velocity of Z (m s^{-1})	0	2	5	9

Which of the following statements is/are correct?

I X moves with constant velocity.
II Y moves with constant acceleration.
III Z moves with constant acceleration.

A I only
B II only
C I and II only
D I and III only
E II and III only

16. A car of mass 1200 kg is travelling along a straight level road at a constant speed of 20 m s^{-1}.

The driving force on the car is 2500 N. The frictional force on the car is 2500 N.

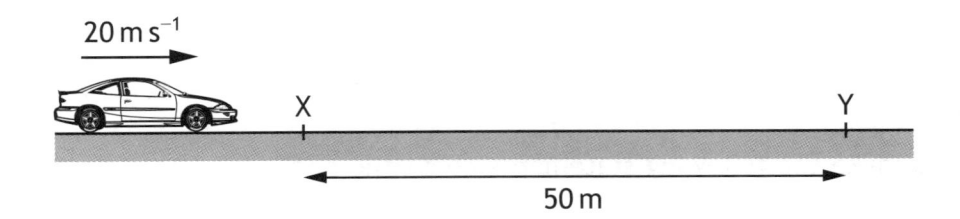

The work done moving the car between point X and point Y is

A 0 J
B 11 800 J
C 125 000 J
D 240 000 J
E 250 000 J.

[Turn over

17. A person sits on a chair which rests on the Earth. The person exerts a downward force on the chair.

Which of the following is the reaction to this force?

A   The force of the chair on the person
B   The force of the person on the chair
C   The force of the Earth on the person
D   The force of the chair on the Earth
E   The force of the person on the Earth

18. A package falls vertically from a helicopter. After some time the package reaches its terminal velocity.

A group of students make the following statements about the package when it reaches its terminal velocity.

I   The weight of the package is less than the air resistance acting on the package.
II The forces acting on the package are balanced.
III The package is accelerating towards the ground at $9 \cdot 8 \, m \, s^{-2}$.

Which of these statements is/are correct?

A   I only
B   II only
C   III only
D   I and III only
E   II and III only

19. The distance from the Sun to Proxima Centauri is 4·3 light years.

    This distance is equivalent to

    A $1·4 \times 10^8$ m
    B $1·6 \times 10^{14}$ m
    C $6·8 \times 10^{14}$ m
    D $9·5 \times 10^{15}$ m
    E $4·1 \times 10^{16}$ m.

20. Light from a star is split into a line spectrum of different colours. The line spectrum from the star is shown, along with the line spectra of the elements calcium, helium, hydrogen and sodium.

    line spectrum from star

    calcium

    helium

    hydrogen

    sodium

    The elements present in this star are

    A   sodium and calcium
    B   calcium and helium
    C   hydrogen and sodium
    D   helium and hydrogen
    E   calcium, sodium and hydrogen.

[END OF SECTION 1. NOW ATTEMPT THE QUESTIONS IN SECTION 2 OF YOUR QUESTION AND ANSWER BOOKLET]

N5

National Qualifications 2015

X757/75/11

**Physics
Relationships Sheet**

TUESDAY, 5 MAY
9:00 AM – 11:00 AM

$$E_p = mgh$$

$$E_k = \tfrac{1}{2}mv^2$$

$$Q = It$$

$$V = IR$$

$$R_T = R_1 + R_2 + \ldots$$

$$\frac{1}{R_T} = \frac{1}{R_1} + \frac{1}{R_2} + \ldots$$

$$V_2 = \left(\frac{R_2}{R_1 + R_2}\right)V_s$$

$$\frac{V_1}{V_2} = \frac{R_1}{R_2}$$

$$P = \frac{E}{t}$$

$$P = IV$$

$$P = I^2 R$$

$$P = \frac{V^2}{R}$$

$$E_h = cm\Delta T$$

$$p = \frac{F}{A}$$

$$\frac{pV}{T} = \text{constant}$$

$$p_1 V_1 = p_2 V_2$$

$$\frac{p_1}{T_1} = \frac{p_2}{T_2}$$

$$\frac{V_1}{T_1} = \frac{V_2}{T_2}$$

$$d = vt$$

$$v = f\lambda$$

$$T = \frac{1}{f}$$

$$A = \frac{N}{t}$$

$$D = \frac{E}{m}$$

$$H = Dw_R$$

$$\dot{H} = \frac{H}{t}$$

$$s = vt$$

$$d = \bar{v}t$$

$$s = \bar{v}t$$

$$a = \frac{v - u}{t}$$

$$W = mg$$

$$F = ma$$

$$E_w = Fd$$

$$E_h = ml$$

Additional Relationships

Circle

circumference = $2\pi r$

area = πr^2

Sphere

area = $4\pi r^2$

volume = $\frac{4}{3}\pi r^3$

Trigonometry

$\sin \theta = \dfrac{\text{opposite}}{\text{hypotenuse}}$

$\cos \theta = \dfrac{\text{adjacent}}{\text{hypotenuse}}$

$\tan \theta = \dfrac{\text{opposite}}{\text{adjacent}}$

$\sin^2 \theta + \cos^2 \theta = 1$

Electron Arrangements of Elements

Key
- Atomic number
- Symbol
- Electron arrangement
- Name

Group 1

1 **H** 1 Hydrogen	
3 **Li** 2,1 Lithium	
11 **Na** 2,8,1 Sodium	
19 **K** 2,8,8,1 Potassium	
37 **Rb** 2,8,18,8,1 Rubidium	
55 **Cs** 2,8,18,18,8,1 Caesium	
87 **Fr** 2,8,18,32,18,8,1 Francium	

Group 2

| 4 **Be** 2,2 Beryllium |
| 12 **Mg** 2,8,2 Magnesium |
| 20 **Ca** 2,8,8,2 Calcium |
| 38 **Sr** 2,8,18,8,2 Strontium |
| 56 **Ba** 2,8,18,18,8,2 Barium |
| 88 **Ra** 2,8,18,32,18,8,2 Radium |

Transition Elements (Groups 3–12)

Group 3	Group 4	Group 5	Group 6	Group 7	Group 8	Group 9	Group 10	Group 11	Group 12
21 **Sc** 2,8,9,2 Scandium	22 **Ti** 2,8,10,2 Titanium	23 **V** 2,8,11,2 Vanadium	24 **Cr** 2,8,13,1 Chromium	25 **Mn** 2,8,13,2 Manganese	26 **Fe** 2,8,14,2 Iron	27 **Co** 2,8,15,2 Cobalt	28 **Ni** 2,8,16,2 Nickel	29 **Cu** 2,8,18,1 Copper	30 **Zn** 2,8,18,2 Zinc
39 **Y** 2,8,18,9,2 Yttrium	40 **Zr** 2,8,18,10,2 Zirconium	41 **Nb** 2,8,18,12,1 Niobium	42 **Mo** 2,8,18,13,1 Molybdenum	43 **Tc** 2,8,18,13,2 Technetium	44 **Ru** 2,8,18,15,1 Ruthenium	45 **Rh** 2,8,18,16,1 Rhodium	46 **Pd** 2,8,18,18,0 Palladium	47 **Ag** 2,8,18,18,1 Silver	48 **Cd** 2,8,18,18,2 Cadmium
57 **La** 2,8,18,18,9,2 Lanthanum	72 **Hf** 2,8,18,32,10,2 Hafnium	73 **Ta** 2,8,18,32,11,2 Tantalum	74 **W** 2,8,18,32,12,2 Tungsten	75 **Re** 2,8,18,32,13,2 Rhenium	76 **Os** 2,8,18,32,14,2 Osmium	77 **Ir** 2,8,18,32,15,2 Iridium	78 **Pt** 2,8,18,32,17,1 Platinum	79 **Au** 2,8,18,32,18,1 Gold	80 **Hg** 2,8,18,32,18,2 Mercury
89 **Ac** 2,8,18,32,18,9,2 Actinium	104 **Rf** 2,8,18,32,32,10,2 Rutherfordium	105 **Db** 2,8,18,32,32,11,2 Dubnium	106 **Sg** 2,8,18,32,32,12,2 Seaborgium	107 **Bh** 2,8,18,32,32,13,2 Bohrium	108 **Hs** 2,8,18,32,32,14,2 Hassium	109 **Mt** 2,8,18,32,32,15,2 Meitnerium	110 **Ds** 2,8,18,32,32,17,1 Darmstadtium	111 **Rg** 2,8,18,32,32,18,1 Roentgenium	112 **Cn** 2,8,18,32,32,18,2 Copernicium

Groups 3–0 (main)

Group 3	Group 4	Group 5	Group 6	Group 7	Group 0
					2 **He** 2 Helium
5 **B** 2,3 Boron	6 **C** 2,4 Carbon	7 **N** 2,5 Nitrogen	8 **O** 2,6 Oxygen	9 **F** 2,7 Fluorine	10 **Ne** 2,8 Neon
13 **Al** 2,8,3 Aluminium	14 **Si** 2,8,4 Silicon	15 **P** 2,8,5 Phosphorus	16 **S** 2,8,6 Sulfur	17 **Cl** 2,8,7 Chlorine	18 **Ar** 2,8,8 Argon
31 **Ga** 2,8,18,3 Gallium	32 **Ge** 2,8,18,4 Germanium	33 **As** 2,8,18,5 Arsenic	34 **Se** 2,8,18,6 Selenium	35 **Br** 2,8,18,7 Bromine	36 **Kr** 2,8,18,8 Krypton
49 **In** 2,8,18,18,3 Indium	50 **Sn** 2,8,18,18,4 Tin	51 **Sb** 2,8,18,18,5 Antimony	52 **Te** 2,8,18,18,6 Tellurium	53 **I** 2,8,18,18,7 Iodine	54 **Xe** 2,8,18,18,8 Xenon
81 **Tl** 2,8,18,32,18,3 Thallium	82 **Pb** 2,8,18,32,18,4 Lead	83 **Bi** 2,8,18,32,18,5 Bismuth	84 **Po** 2,8,18,32,18,6 Polonium	85 **At** 2,8,18,32,18,7 Astatine	86 **Rn** 2,8,18,32,18,8 Radon

Lanthanides

| 57 **La** 2,8,18,18,9,2 Lanthanum | 58 **Ce** 2,8,18,20,8,2 Cerium | 59 **Pr** 2,8,18,21,8,2 Praseodymium | 60 **Nd** 2,8,18,22,8,2 Neodymium | 61 **Pm** 2,8,18,23,8,2 Promethium | 62 **Sm** 2,8,18,24,8,2 Samarium | 63 **Eu** 2,8,18,25,8,2 Europium | 64 **Gd** 2,8,18,25,9,2 Gadolinium | 65 **Tb** 2,8,18,27,8,2 Terbium | 66 **Dy** 2,8,18,28,8,2 Dysprosium | 67 **Ho** 2,8,18,29,8,2 Holmium | 68 **Er** 2,8,18,30,8,2 Erbium | 69 **Tm** 2,8,18,31,8,2 Thulium | 70 **Yb** 2,8,18,32,8,2 Ytterbium | 71 **Lu** 2,8,18,32,9,2 Lutetium |

Actinides

| 89 **Ac** 2,8,18,32,18,9,2 Actinium | 90 **Th** 2,8,18,32,18,10,2 Thorium | 91 **Pa** 2,8,18,32,20,9,2 Protactinium | 92 **U** 2,8,18,32,21,9,2 Uranium | 93 **Np** 2,8,18,32,22,9,2 Neptunium | 94 **Pu** 2,8,18,32,24,8,2 Plutonium | 95 **Am** 2,8,18,32,25,8,2 Americium | 96 **Cm** 2,8,18,32,25,9,2 Curium | 97 **Bk** 2,8,18,32,27,8,2 Berkelium | 98 **Cf** 2,8,18,32,28,8,2 Californium | 99 **Es** 2,8,18,32,29,8,2 Einsteinium | 100 **Fm** 2,8,18,32,30,8,2 Fermium | 101 **Md** 2,8,18,32,31,8,2 Mendelevium | 102 **No** 2,8,18,32,32,8,2 Nobelium | 103 **Lr** 2,8,18,32,32,9,2 Lawrencium |

N5

FOR OFFICIAL USE

National Qualifications 2015

Mark

X757/75/01

Physics
Section 1—Answer Grid and Section 2

TUESDAY, 5 MAY
9:00 AM – 11:00 AM

Fill in these boxes and read what is printed below.

Full name of centre

Town

Forename(s)

Surname

Number of seat

Date of birth
Day Month Year

Scottish candidate number

Total marks — 110

SECTION 1 — 20 marks
Attempt ALL questions.
Instructions for the completion of Section 1 are given on *Page two*.

SECTION 2 — 90 marks
Attempt ALL questions.

Reference may be made to the Data Sheet on *Page two* of the question paper X757/75/02 and to the Relationship Sheet X757/75/11.

Care should be taken to give an appropriate number of significant figures in the final answers to calculations.

Write your answers clearly in the spaces provided in this booklet. Additional space for answers and rough work is provided at the end of this booklet. If you use this space you must clearly identify the question number you are attempting. Any rough work must be written in this booklet. You should score through your rough work when you have written your final copy.

Use **blue** or **black** ink.

Before leaving the examination room you must give this booklet to the Invigilator; if you do not, you may lose all the marks for this paper.

SQA

SECTION 1 — 20 marks

The questions for Section 1 are contained in the question paper X757/75/02.
Read these and record your answers on the answer grid on *Page three* opposite.
Use **blue** or **black** ink. Do NOT use gel pens or pencil.

1. The answer to each question is **either** A, B, C, D or E. Decide what your answer is, then fill in the appropriate bubble (see sample question below).

2. There is **only one correct** answer to each question.

3. Any rough work must be written in the additional space for answers and rough work at the end of this booklet.

Sample Question

The energy unit measured by the electricity meter in your home is the:

  A   ampere

  B   kilowatt-hour

  C   watt

  D   coulomb

  E   volt.

The correct answer is **B** — kilowatt-hour. The answer **B** bubble has been clearly filled in (see below).

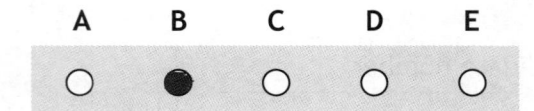

Changing an answer

If you decide to change your answer, cancel your first answer by putting a cross through it (see below) and fill in the answer you want. The answer below has been changed to **D**.

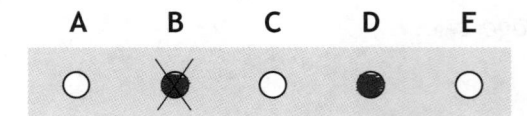

If you then decide to change back to an answer you have already scored out, put a tick (✓) to the **right** of the answer you want, as shown below:

SECTION 1 — Answer Grid

	A	B	C	D	E
1	○	○	○	○	○
2	○	○	○	○	○
3	○	○	○	○	○
4	○	○	○	○	○
5	○	○	○	○	○
6	○	○	○	○	○
7	○	○	○	○	○
8	○	○	○	○	○
9	○	○	○	○	○
10	○	○	○	○	○
11	○	○	○	○	○
12	○	○	○	○	○
13	○	○	○	○	○
14	○	○	○	○	○
15	○	○	○	○	○
16	○	○	○	○	○
17	○	○	○	○	○
18	○	○	○	○	○
19	○	○	○	○	○
20	○	○	○	○	○

[Turn over for Question 1 on *Page six*

DO NOT WRITE ON THIS PAGE

SECTION 2 — 90 marks

Attempt ALL questions

1. A student sets up the following circuit using a battery, two lamps, a switch and a resistor.

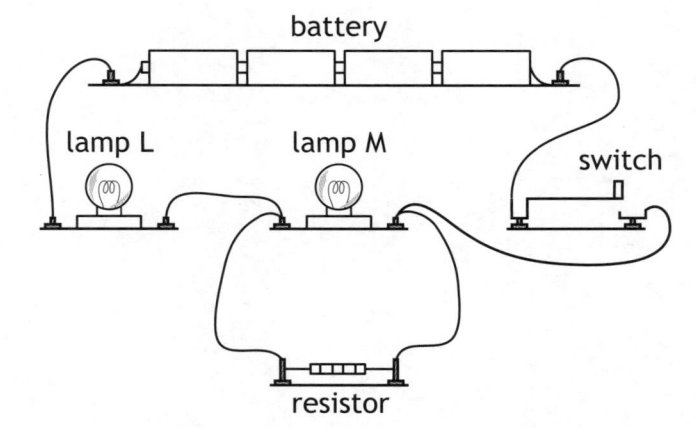

    (a) Draw a circuit diagram for this circuit using the correct symbols for the components. **3**

    (b) Each lamp is rated 2·5 V, 0·50 A.

    Calculate the resistance of one of the lamps when it is operating at the correct voltage. **3**

    Space for working and answer

1. (continued)

(c) When the switch is closed, will lamp L be brighter, dimmer or the same brightness as lamp M?

You **must** justify your answer.   **3**

[Turn over

2. (a) A student investigates the electrical properties of three different components; a lamp, an LED and a fixed resistor.

Current-voltage graphs produced from the student's results are shown.

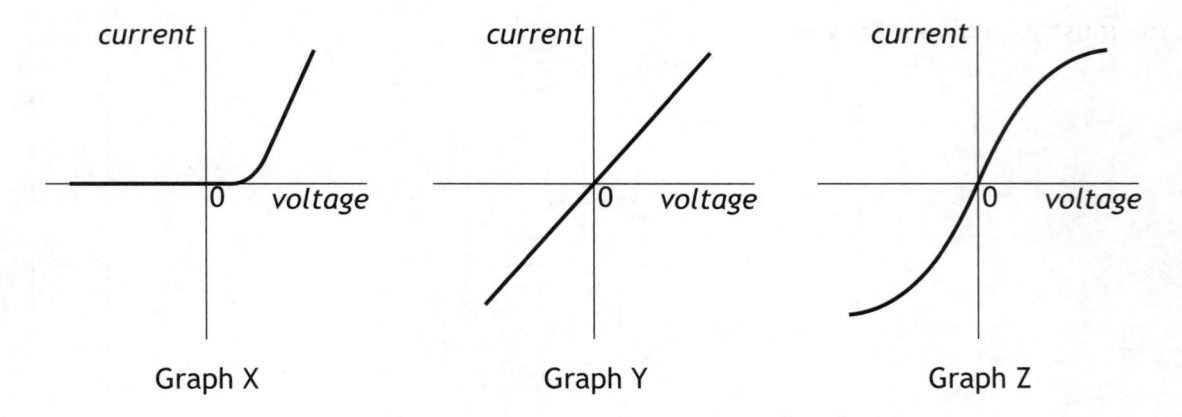

Graph X   Graph Y   Graph Z

Explain which graph X, Y or Z is obtained from the student's results for the LED. **2**

(b) One of the components is operated at 4·0 V with a current of 0·50 A for 60 seconds.

(i) Calculate the energy transferred to the component during this time. **4**

Space for working and answer

2. (b) (continued)

(ii) Calculate the charge which passes through this component during this time.

Space for working and answer

3

[Turn over

3. A technician uses pulses of ultrasound (high frequency sound) to detect imperfections in a sample of steel.

The pulses of ultrasound are transmitted into the steel.

The speed of ultrasound in steel is 5200 m s^{-1}.

Where there are no imperfections, the pulses of ultrasound travel through the steel and are reflected by the back wall of the steel.

Where there are imperfections in the steel, the pulses of ultrasound are reflected by these imperfections.

The reflected pulses return through the sample and are detected by the ultrasound receiver.

The technician transmits pulses of ultrasound into the steel at positions X, Y and Z as shown.

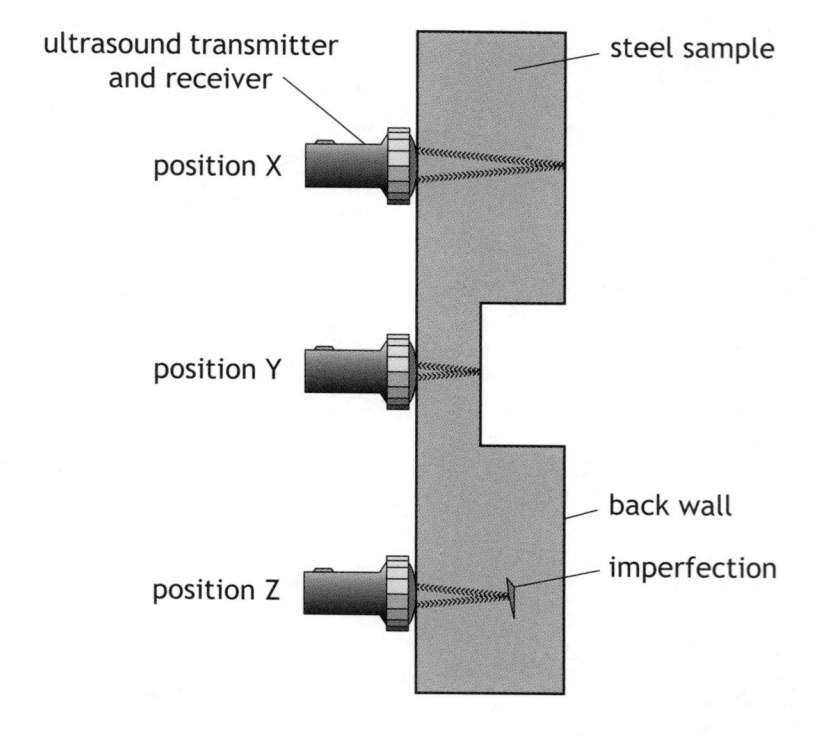

The times between the pulses being transmitted and received for positions X and Y are shown in the graph.

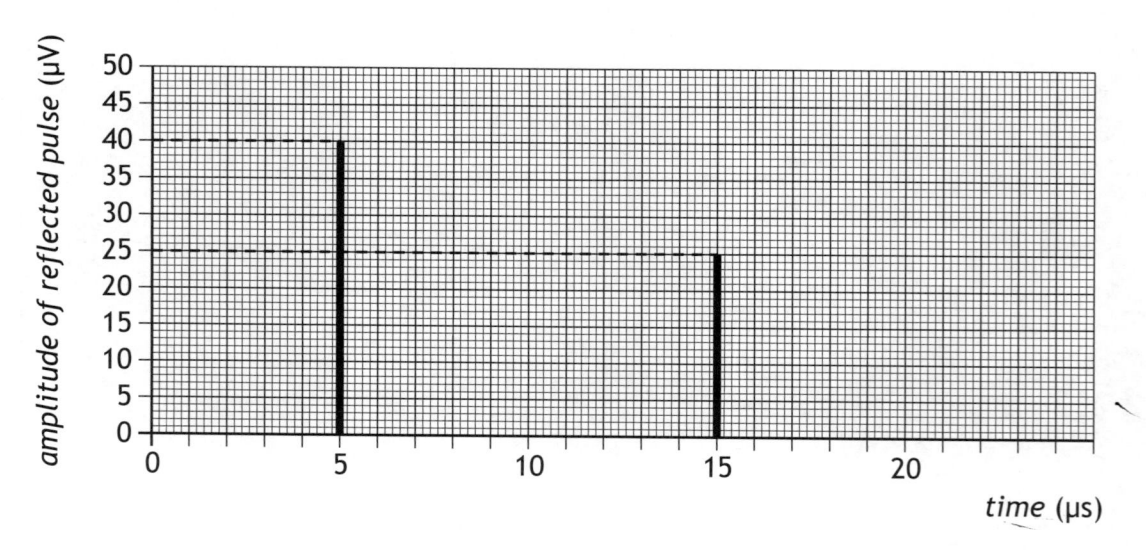

3. (continued)

(a) (i) State the time taken between the pulse being transmitted and received at position X. **1**

(ii) Calculate the thickness of the steel sample at position X. **4**

Space for working and answer

(b) On the graph on the previous page, draw a line to show the reflected pulse from position Z. **2**

(c) The ultrasound pulses used have a period of 4·0 μs.

(i) Show that the frequency of the ultrasound pulses is $2·5 \times 10^5$ Hz. **2**

Space for working and answer

(ii) Calculate the wavelength of the ultrasound pulses in the steel sample. **3**

Space for working and answer

3. (continued)

(d) The technician replaces the steel sample with a brass sample.

The brass sample has the same thickness as the steel sample at position X.

The technician transmits pulses of ultrasound into the brass at position P as shown.

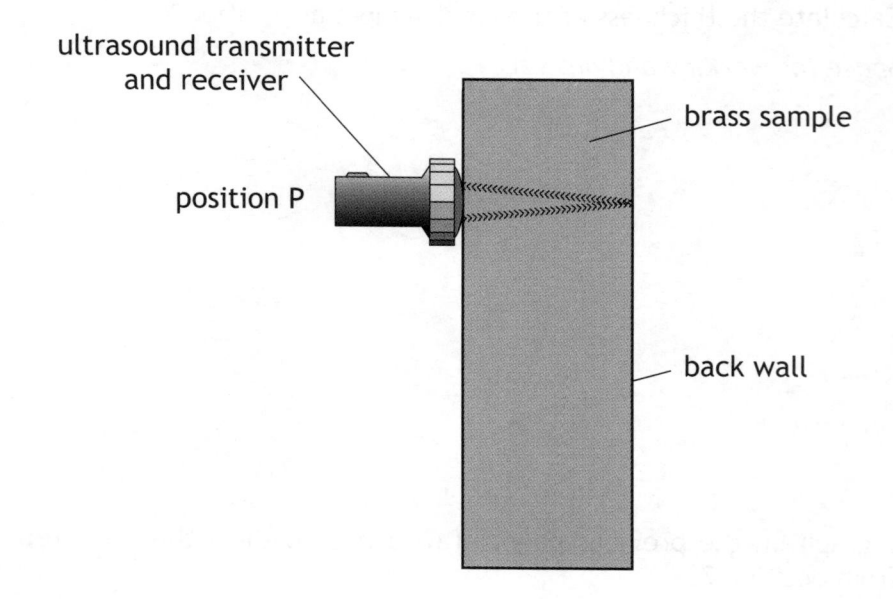

The time between the ultrasound pulse being transmitted and received at position P is greater than the time recorded at position X in the steel sample.

State whether the speed of ultrasound in brass is less than, equal to or greater than the speed of ultrasound in steel.

You **must** justify your answer.

2

MARKS 3

4. A science technician removes two metal blocks from an oven. Immediately after the blocks are removed from the oven the technician measures the temperature of each block, using an infrared thermometer. The temperature of each block is 230 °C.

After several minutes the temperature of each block is measured again. One block is now at a temperature of 123 °C and the other block is at a temperature of 187 °C.

Using your knowledge of physics, comment on possible explanations for this difference in temperature.

[Turn over

5. Diamonds are popular and sought after gemstones.

Light is refracted as it enters and leaves a diamond.

The diagram shows a ray of light entering a diamond.

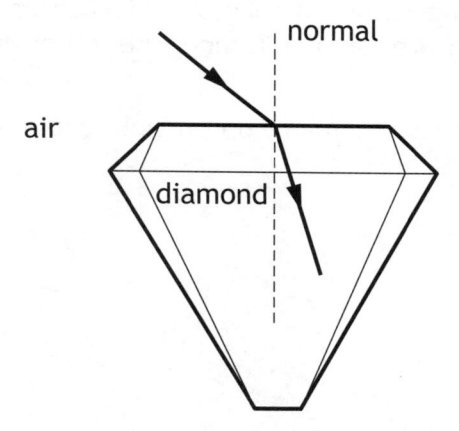

(a) On the diagram, label the angle of incidence *i* and the angle of refraction *r*. **1**

(b) State what happens to the speed of the light as it enters the diamond. **1**

(c) The optical density of a gemstone is a measure of its ability to refract light.

Gemstones of higher optical density cause more refraction.

A ray of light is directed into a gemstone at an angle of incidence of 45°.

The angle of refraction is then measured.

This is repeated for different gemstones.

Gemstone	Angle of refraction
A	24·3°
B	17·0°
C	27·3°
D	19·0°
E	25·5°

Diamond is known to have the highest optical density.

Identify which gemstone is most likely to be diamond. **1**

5. (continued)

   (d) Diamond is one of the hardest known substances.

   Synthetic diamonds are attached to the cutting edges of drill bits for use in the oil industry.

   These drill bits are able to cut into rock.

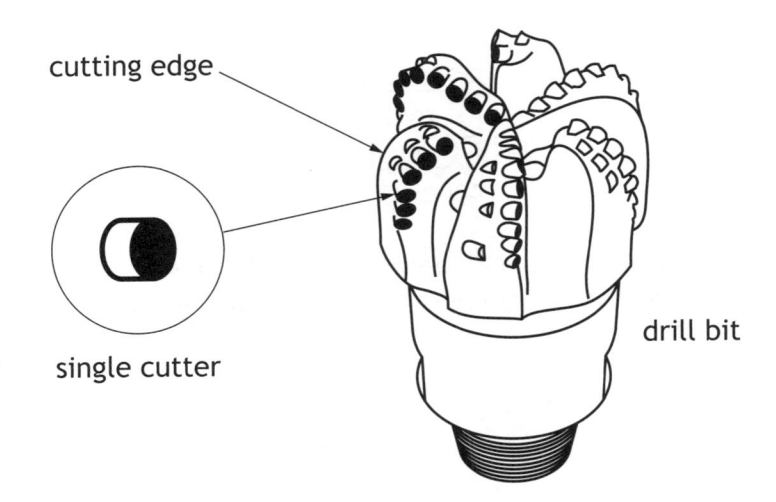

   The area of a single cutter in contact with the rock is $1.1 \times 10^{-5}\,m^2$.

   When drilling, this cutter is designed to exert a maximum force of 61 kN on the rock.

   Calculate the maximum pressure that the cutter can exert on the rock.

   Space for working and answer

[Turn over

6. A paper mill uses a radioactive source in a system to monitor the thickness of paper.

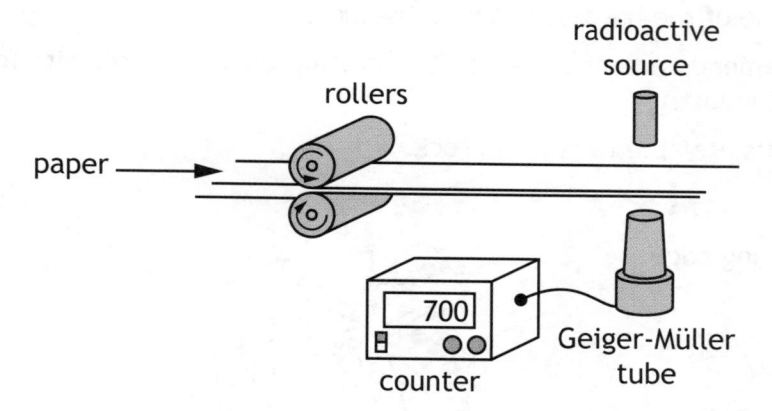

Radiation passing through the paper is detected by the Geiger-Müller tube. The count rate is displayed on the counter as shown. The radioactive source has a half-life that allows the system to run continuously.

(a) State what happens to the count rate if the thickness of the paper decreases.

(b) The following radioactive sources are available.

Radioactive Source	Half-life	Radiation emitted
W	600 years	alpha
X	50 years	beta
Y	4 hours	beta
Z	350 years	gamma

(i) State which radioactive source should be used.
You **must** explain your answer.

6. (b) (continued)

(ii) State what is meant by the term *half-life*. **1**

(iii) State what is meant by a gamma ray. **1**

(c) The graph below shows how the activity of another radioactive source varies with time.

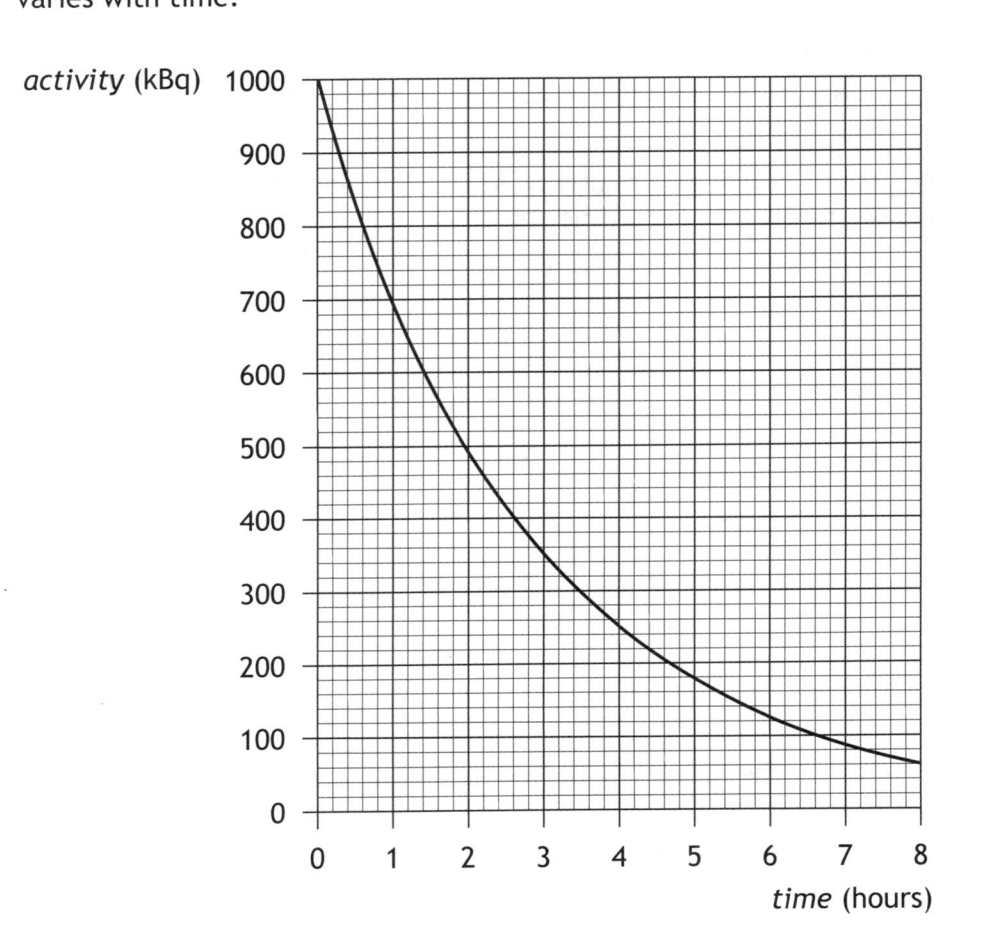

Determine the half-life of this radioactive source. **1**

[Turn over

7. A ship of mass 5.0×10^6 kg leaves a port. Its engine produces a forward force of 8.0×10^3 N. A tugboat pushes against one side of the ship as shown. The tugboat applies a pushing force of 6.0×10^3 N.

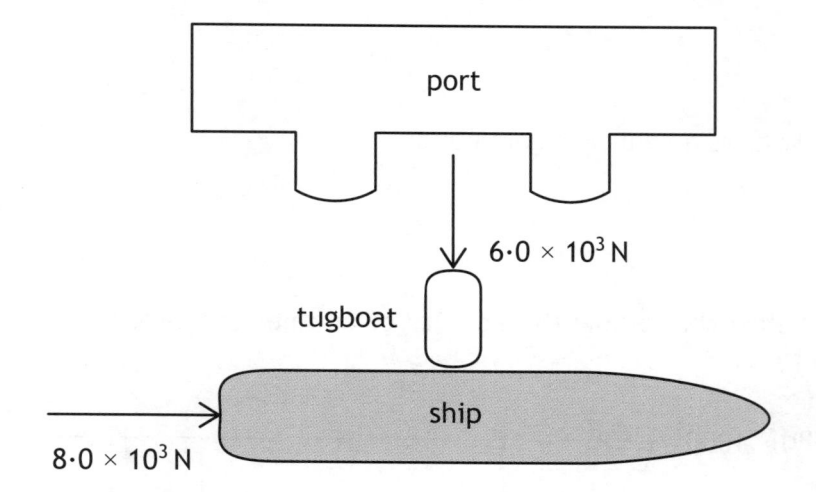

(a) (i) By scale drawing, or otherwise, determine the size of the resultant force acting on the ship.

Space for working and answer

(ii) Determine the direction of the resultant force relative to the 8.0×10^3 N force.

Space for working and answer

7. (a) (continued)

(iii) Calculate the size of the acceleration of the ship.   3

Space for working and answer

(b) Out in the open sea the ship comes to rest.

Explain, with the aid of a labelled diagram, why the ship floats.   3

[Turn over

8. A student is investigating the motion of a trolley down a ramp.

(a) The student uses the apparatus shown to carry out an experiment to determine the acceleration of a trolley as it rolls down a ramp.

The trolley is released from rest at the top of the ramp.

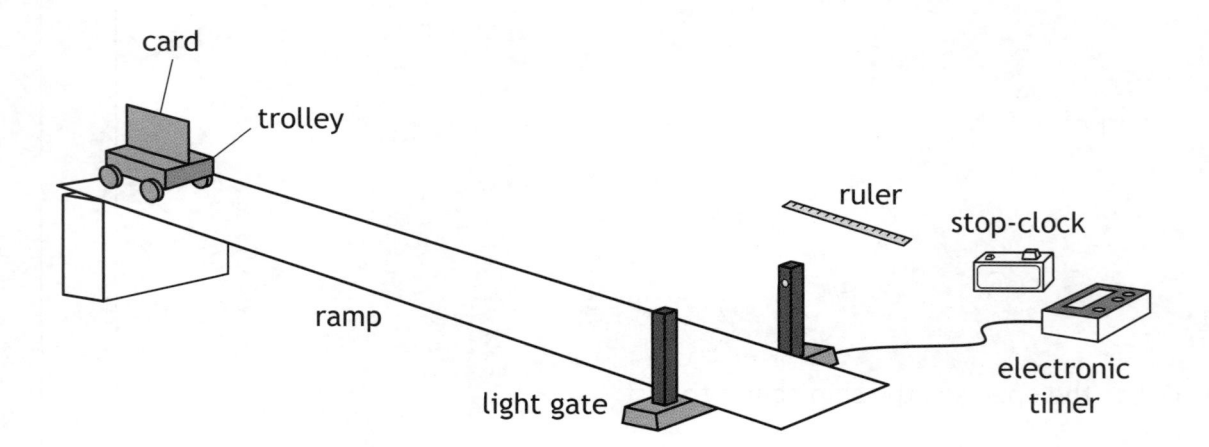

(i) State the measurements the student must make to calculate the acceleration of the trolley. **3**

(ii) Suggest one reason why the acceleration calculated from these measurements might not be accurate. **1**

8. (continued)

(b) In a second experiment, the student uses a motion sensor and computer to produce the following velocity-time graph for the trolley

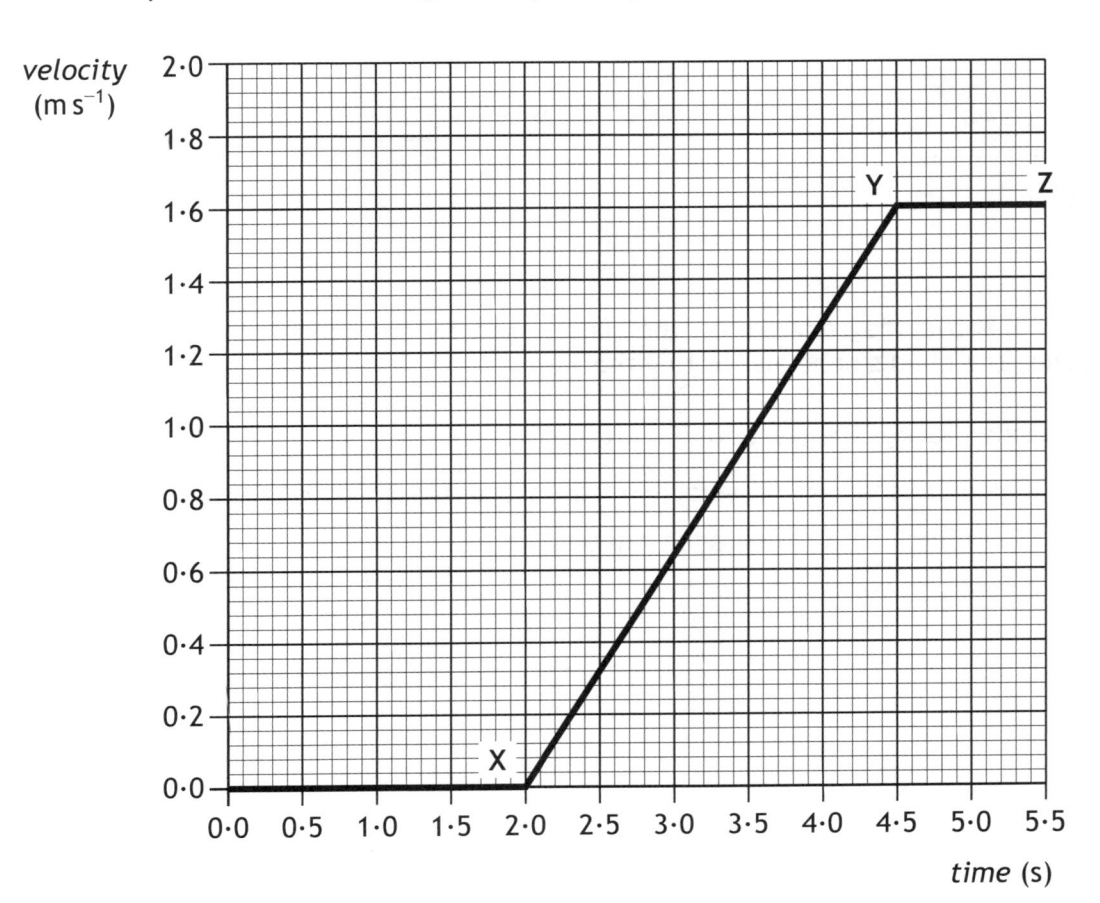

Calculate the acceleration of this trolley between X and Y.

Space for working and answer

9. A child throws a stone horizontally from a bridge into a river.

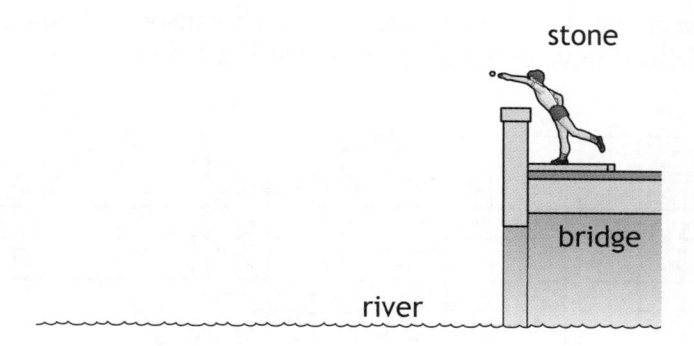

(a) On the above diagram sketch the path taken by the stone between leaving the child's hand and hitting the water. **1**

(b) The stone reaches the water 0·80 s after it was released.

  (i) Calculate the vertical velocity of the stone as it reaches the water.
  The effects of air resistance can be ignored. **3**

  Space for working and answer

  (ii) Determine the height above the water at which the stone was released. **4**

  Space for working and answer

(c) The child now drops a similar stone vertically from the same height into the river.

State how the time taken for this stone to reach the water compares with the time taken for the stone in (b). **1**

10. Space exploration involves placing astronauts in difficult environments. Despite this, many people believe the benefits of space exploration outweigh the risks.

Using your knowledge of physics, comment on the benefits and/or risks of space exploration.

3

[Turn over

11. Craters on the Moon are caused by meteors striking its surface.

A student investigates how a crater is formed by dropping a marble into a tray of sand.

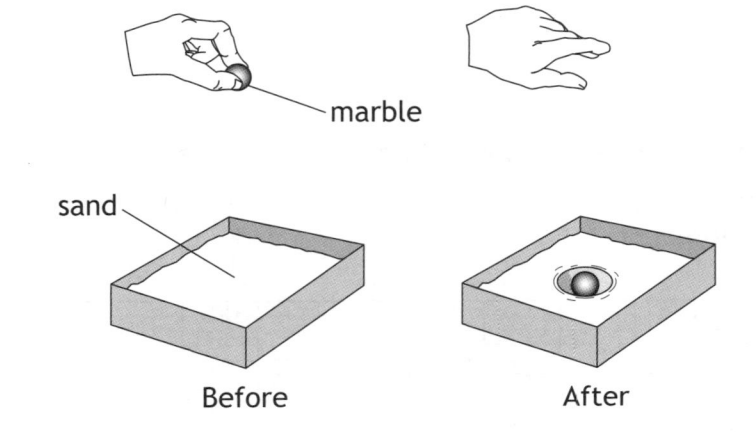

Before   After

(a) The marble has a mass of 0·040 kg.

(i) Calculate the loss in potential energy of the marble when it is dropped from a height of 0·50 m. **3**

Space for working and answer

(ii) Describe the energy change that takes place as the marble hits the sand. **1**

[Turn over

11. (continued)

(b) The student drops the marble from different heights and measures the diameter of each crater that is formed.

The table shows the student's results.

height (m)	diameter (m)
0·05	0·030
0·10	0·044
0·15	0·053
0·35	0·074
0·40	0·076
0·45	0·076

(i) Using the graph paper below, draw a graph of these results.

(Additional graph paper, if required, can be found on *Page twenty-eight*)

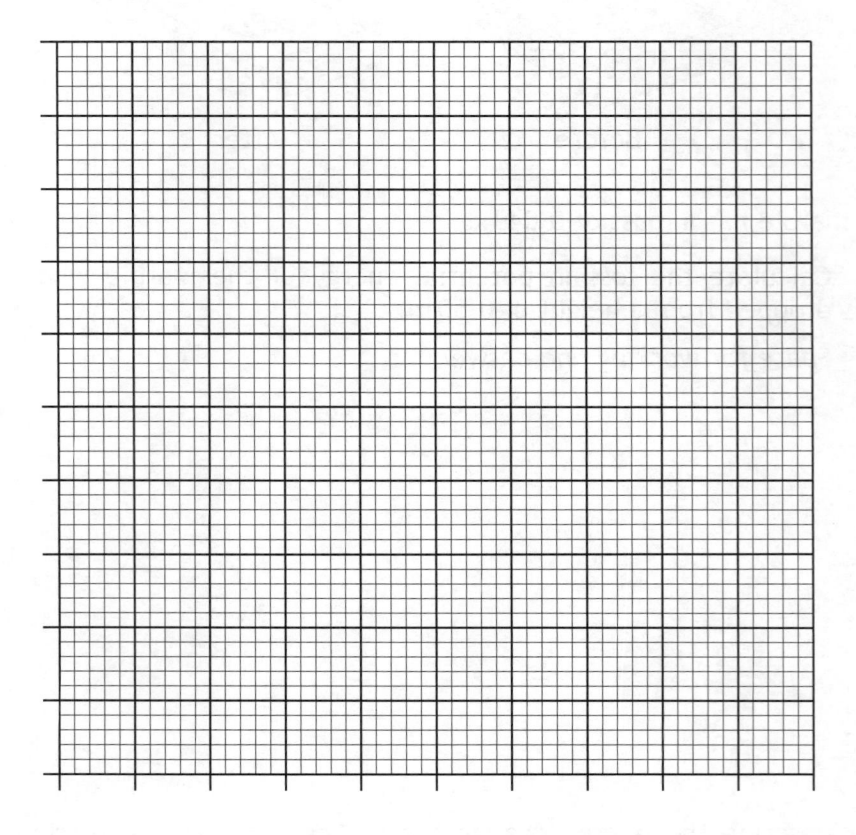

11. (b) (continued)

(ii) Use your graph to predict the diameter of the crater that is formed when the marble is dropped from a height of 0·25 m. **1**

(iii) Suggest two improvements that the student could make to this investigation. **2**

(c) (i) Suggest another variable, which could be investigated, that may affect the diameter of a crater. **1**

(ii) Describe experimental work that could be carried out to investigate how this variable affects the diameter of a crater. **2**

[END OF QUESTION PAPER]

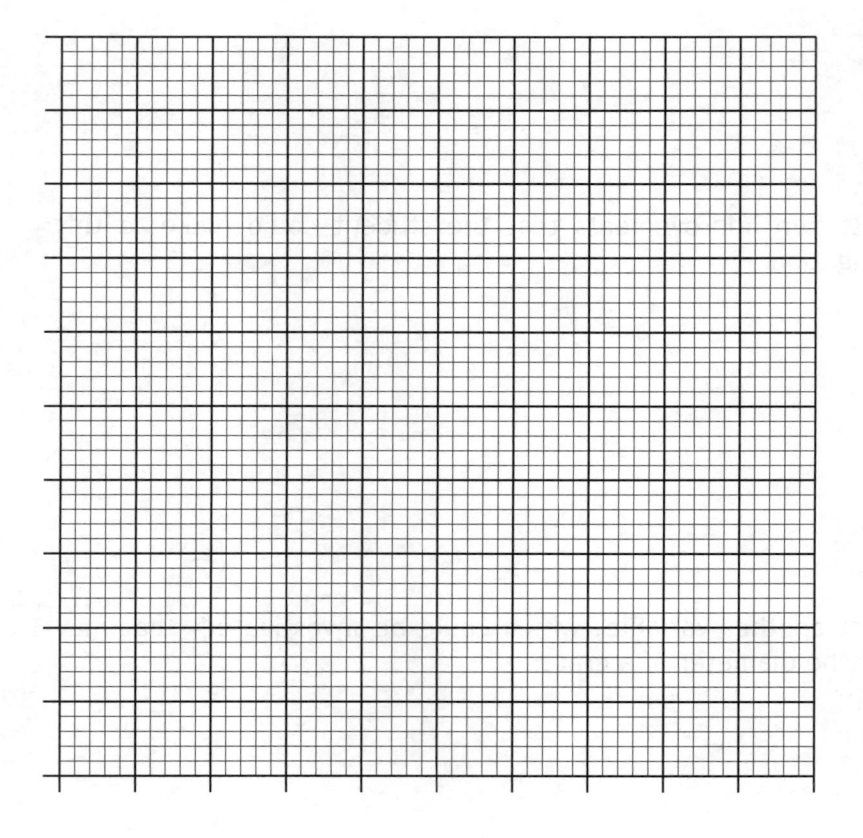

ADDITIONAL SPACE FOR ANSWERS AND ROUGH WORKING

Additional graph paper for Q11 (b) (i)

ADDITIONAL SPACE FOR ANSWERS AND ROUGH WORKING

ADDITIONAL SPACE FOR ANSWERS AND ROUGH WORKING

NATIONAL 5
2017

N5 National Qualifications 2017

X757/75/02

**Physics
Section 1—Questions**

WEDNESDAY, 17 MAY
1:00 PM — 3:00 PM

Instructions for the completion of Section 1 are given on *Page two* of your question and answer booklet X757/75/01.

Record your answers on the answer grid on *Page three* of your question and answer booklet.

Reference may be made to the Data Sheet on *Page two* of this booklet and to the Relationship Sheet X757/75/11.

Before leaving the examination room you must give your question and answer booklet to the Invigilator; if you do not, you may lose all the marks for this paper.

SQA

DATA SHEET

Speed of light in materials

Material	Speed in m s^{-1}
Air	3.0×10^8
Carbon dioxide	3.0×10^8
Diamond	1.2×10^8
Glass	2.0×10^8
Glycerol	2.1×10^8
Water	2.3×10^8

Speed of sound in materials

Material	Speed in m s^{-1}
Aluminium	5200
Air	340
Bone	4100
Carbon dioxide	270
Glycerol	1900
Muscle	1600
Steel	5200
Tissue	1500
Water	1500

Gravitational field strengths

	Gravitational field strength on the surface in N kg^{-1}
Earth	9.8
Jupiter	23
Mars	3.7
Mercury	3.7
Moon	1.6
Neptune	11
Saturn	9.0
Sun	270
Uranus	8.7
Venus	8.9

Specific heat capacity of materials

Material	Specific heat capacity in J kg^{-1} °C^{-1}
Alcohol	2350
Aluminium	902
Copper	386
Glass	500
Ice	2100
Iron	480
Lead	128
Oil	2130
Water	4180

Specific latent heat of fusion of materials

Material	Specific latent heat of fusion in J kg^{-1}
Alcohol	0.99×10^5
Aluminium	3.95×10^5
Carbon Dioxide	1.80×10^5
Copper	2.05×10^5
Iron	2.67×10^5
Lead	0.25×10^5
Water	3.34×10^5

Melting and boiling points of materials

Material	Melting point in °C	Boiling point in °C
Alcohol	−98	65
Aluminium	660	2470
Copper	1077	2567
Glycerol	18	290
Lead	328	1737
Iron	1537	2737

Radiation weighting factors

Type of radiation	Radiation weighting factor
alpha	20
beta	1
fast neutrons	10
gamma	1
slow neutrons	3
X-rays	1

Specific latent heat of vaporisation of materials

Material	Specific latent heat of vaporisation in J kg^{-1}
Alcohol	11.2×10^5
Carbon Dioxide	3.77×10^5
Glycerol	8.30×10^5
Turpentine	2.90×10^5
Water	22.6×10^5

SECTION 1

Attempt ALL questions

1. A cyclist is travelling along a straight road. The graph shows how the velocity of the cyclist varies with time.

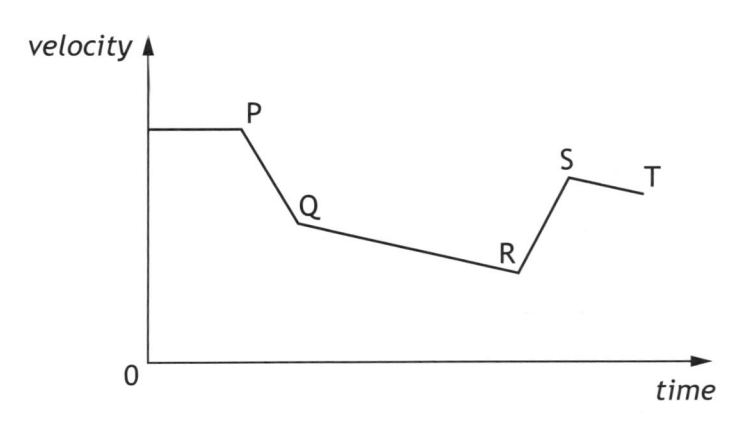

   The kinetic energy of the cyclist is greatest at

   A P
   B Q
   C R
   D S
   E T.

2. A circuit is set up as shown.

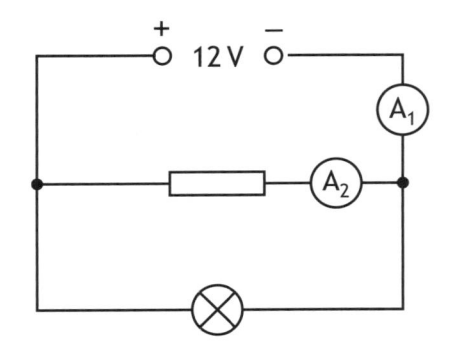

   The reading on ammeter A₁ is 5·0 A. The reading on ammeter A₂ is 2·0 A.
   The charge passing through the lamp in 30 seconds is

   A 0·1 C
   B 10 C
   C 60 C
   D 90 C
   E 150 C.

Page three

[Turn over

3. A lamp is connected to a constant voltage power supply. The power supply is switched on. The graph shows how the current in the lamp varies with time.

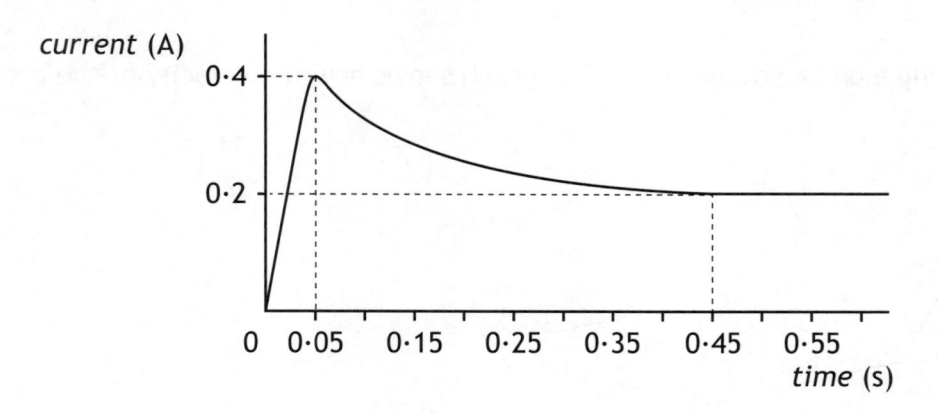

Which row in the table shows what happens to the current and resistance of the lamp between 0·05 s and 0·45 s?

	Current	Resistance
A	decreases	increases
B	decreases	stays the same
C	stays the same	decreases
D	increases	decreases
E	increases	increases

4. A circuit is set up as shown.

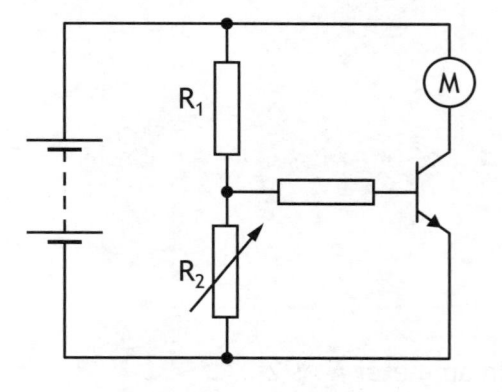

The purpose of the transistor is to

- A supply energy to the circuit
- B decrease the voltage across R_1
- C change electrical energy to kinetic energy
- D supply energy to the motor
- E switch on the motor.

5. Five students each carry out an experiment to determine the specific heat capacity of copper. The setup used by each student is shown.

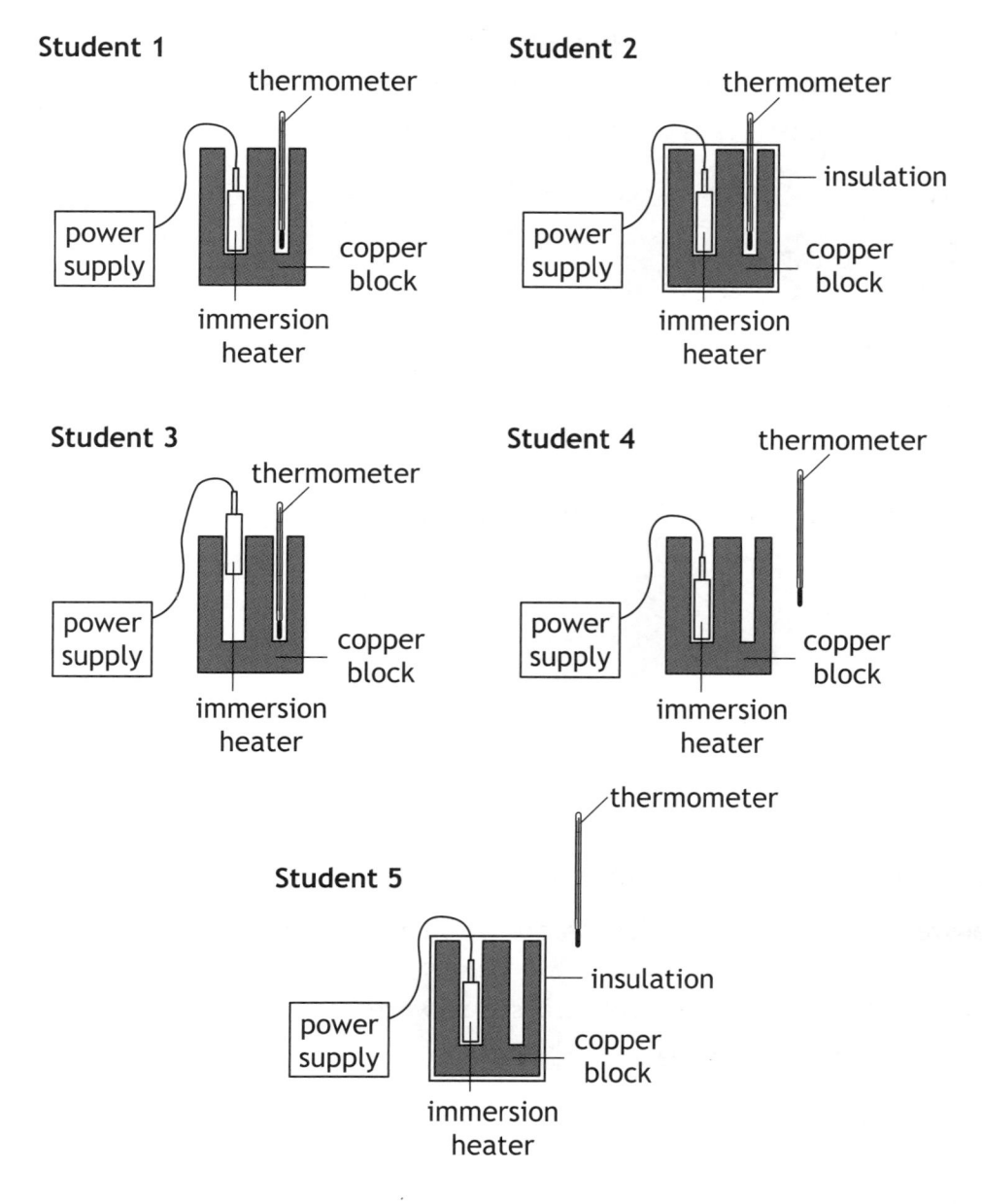

The student with the setup that would allow the most accurate value for the specific heat capacity of copper to be determined is

A   student 1
B   student 2
C   student 3
D   student 4
E   student 5.

6. The mass of a spacecraft is 1200 kg.

   The spacecraft lands on the surface of a planet.

   The gravitational field strength on the surface of the planet is $5\cdot0\,\text{N kg}^{-1}$.

   The spacecraft rests on three pads. The total area of the three pads is $1\cdot5\,\text{m}^2$.

   The pressure exerted by these pads on the surface of the planet is

   A $1\cdot2 \times 10^4\,\text{Pa}$

   B $9\cdot0 \times 10^3\,\text{Pa}$

   C $7\cdot8 \times 10^3\,\text{Pa}$

   D $4\cdot0 \times 10^3\,\text{Pa}$

   E $8\cdot0 \times 10^2\,\text{Pa}$.

7. A solid is heated from $-15\,°\text{C}$ to $60\,°\text{C}$. The temperature change of the solid is

   A   45 K

   B   75 K

   C   258 K

   D   318 K

   E   348 K.

8. A student makes the following statements about waves.

   I   In a transverse wave, the particles vibrate parallel to the direction of travel of the wave.

   II   Light waves and water waves are both transverse waves.

   III   Sound waves are longitudinal waves.

   Which of these statements is/are correct?

   A   I only

   B   II only

   C   III only

   D   I and II only

   E   II and III only

9. The diagram represents a wave travelling from X to Y.

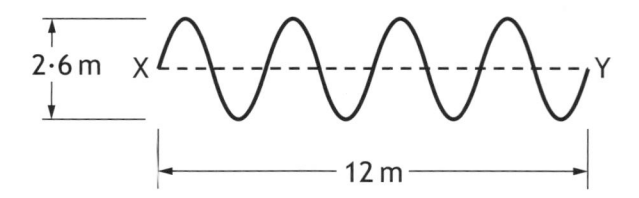

The wave travels from X to Y in a time of 0·5 s.

Which row in the table shows the amplitude, wavelength and frequency of this wave?

	Amplitude (m)	Wavelength (m)	Frequency (Hz)
A	1·3	1·5	2·0
B	2·6	1·5	24
C	1·3	3·0	8·0
D	2·6	3·0	8·0
E	1·3	3·0	24

10. A microwave signal is transmitted by a radar station.

The signal is reflected from an aeroplane.

The aeroplane is at a height of 30 km directly above the radar station.

The time between the signal being transmitted and the reflected signal being received back at the radar station is

A 5×10^{-5} s

B 1×10^{-4} s

C 2×10^{-4} s

D 5×10^{3} s

E 1×10^{4} s.

11. A member of the electromagnetic spectrum has a shorter wavelength than visible light and a lower frequency than X-rays. This type of radiation is

    A gamma
    B ultraviolet
    C infrared
    D microwaves
    E radio waves.

12. The diagram shows the path of a ray of red light as it passes from air into a glass block.

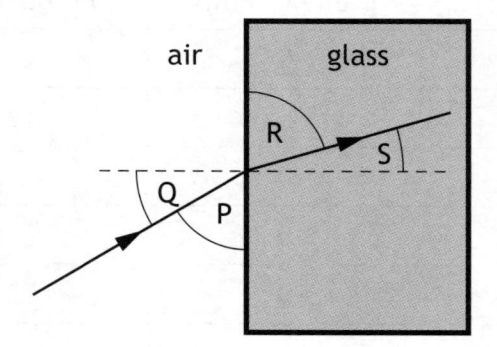

    Which row in the table shows the angle of incidence and the angle of refraction?

	Angle of incidence	Angle of refraction
A	Q	S
B	S	Q
C	P	R
D	R	P
E	Q	R

13. A sample of tissue is exposed to 15 µGy of alpha radiation and 20 µGy of gamma radiation.
    The total equivalent dose received by the tissue is

    A   35 µSv
    B   320 µSv
    C   415 µSv
    D   700 µSv
    E   735 µSv.

14. Two forces act on an object as shown.

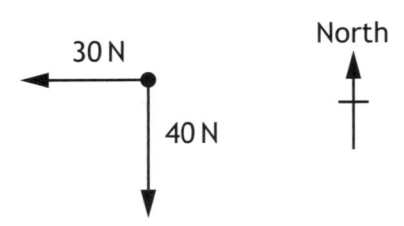

    The resultant force acting on the object is

    A   50 N at a bearing of 053
    B   50 N at a bearing of 143
    C   50 N at a bearing of 217
    D   50 N at a bearing of 233
    E   50 N at a bearing of 323.

15. The graph shows how the velocity v of an object varies with time t.

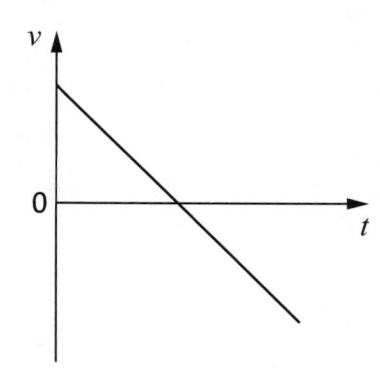

The graph could represent the motion of

A   a ball falling freely downwards

B   a rocket accelerating upwards

C   a ball thrown into the air then falling back to Earth

D   a ball falling to Earth from rest then rebounding upwards again

E   a car slowing to a halt then accelerating in the same direction.

16. A trolley is released from rest at point X and moves with constant acceleration on a slope as shown.

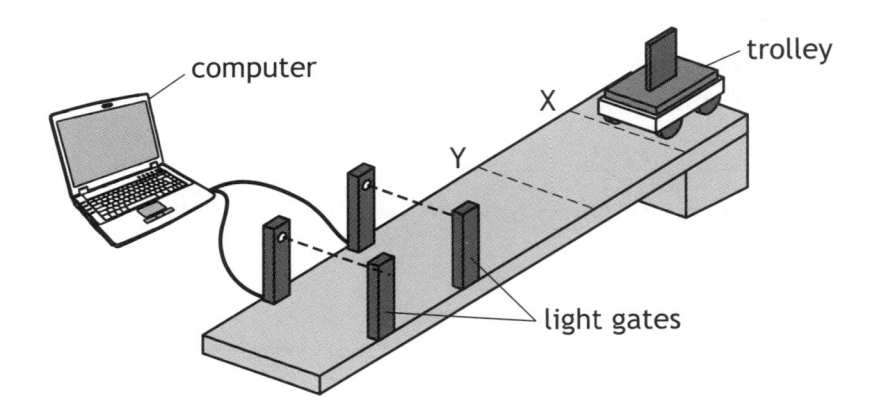

The computer displays the acceleration and average velocity of the trolley between the light gates.

The trolley is now released from rest at point Y.

Which row in the table shows how the acceleration and average velocity compare with the previous results obtained?

	Acceleration	Average velocity
A	less	same
B	same	same
C	greater	greater
D	less	less
E	same	less

17. A rocket accelerates vertically upwards from the surface of the Earth.

   An identical rocket accelerates vertically upwards from the surface of Mars.

   The engine thrust from each rocket is the same.

   Which row in the table shows how the weight of the rocket and the unbalanced force acting on the rocket compares on Mars and Earth?

	Weight on Mars compared to weight on Earth	Unbalanced force on Mars compared to unbalanced force on Earth
A	greater	greater
B	same	same
C	same	less
D	less	greater
E	less	less

18. A satellite is in a circular orbit around a planet.

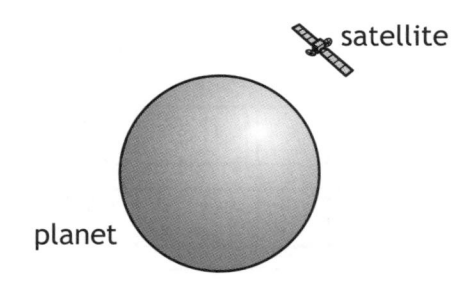

A group of students make the following statements about the satellite.

I   The greater the altitude of a satellite the shorter its orbital period.
II The satellite has a constant vertical acceleration.
III As the satellite orbits the planet, its vertical velocity increases.

Which of these statements is/are correct?

A   I only
B   II only
C   III only
D   I and II only
E   II and III only

19. A heater transfers energy to boiling water at the rate of 1130 joules every second.

The maximum mass of water converted to steam in 2 minutes is

A 1.0×10^{-3} kg
B 6.0×10^{-2} kg
C   0·41 kg
D   17 kg
E   32 kg.

20. Light from stars can be split into line spectra of different colours.

    The line spectra from three stars, X, Y and Z, are shown, along with the line spectra of the elements helium and hydrogen.

    Hydrogen and helium are both present in

    A star X only
    B star Y only
    C stars X and Y only
    D stars X and Z only
    E stars X, Y and Z.

[END OF SECTION 1. NOW ATTEMPT THE QUESTIONS IN SECTION 2 OF YOUR QUESTION AND ANSWER BOOKLET]

[BLANK PAGE]

DO NOT WRITE ON THIS PAGE

N5

National Qualifications 2017

X757/75/11

**Physics
Relationships Sheet**

WEDNESDAY, 17 MAY

1:00 PM – 3:00 PM

$$E_p = mgh$$

$$E_k = \tfrac{1}{2}mv^2$$

$$Q = It$$

$$V = IR$$

$$R_T = R_1 + R_2 + \ldots$$

$$\frac{1}{R_T} = \frac{1}{R_1} + \frac{1}{R_2} + \ldots$$

$$V_2 = \left(\frac{R_2}{R_1 + R_2}\right) V_s$$

$$\frac{V_1}{V_2} = \frac{R_1}{R_2}$$

$$P = \frac{E}{t}$$

$$P = IV$$

$$P = I^2 R$$

$$P = \frac{V^2}{R}$$

$$E_h = cm\Delta T$$

$$p = \frac{F}{A}$$

$$\frac{pV}{T} = \text{constant}$$

$$p_1 V_1 = p_2 V_2$$

$$\frac{p_1}{T_1} = \frac{p_2}{T_2}$$

$$\frac{V_1}{T_1} = \frac{V_2}{T_2}$$

$$d = vt$$

$$v = f\lambda$$

$$T = \frac{1}{f}$$

$$A = \frac{N}{t}$$

$$D = \frac{E}{m}$$

$$H = D w_R$$

$$\dot{H} = \frac{H}{t}$$

$$s = vt$$

$$d = \bar{v} t$$

$$s = \bar{v} t$$

$$a = \frac{v - u}{t}$$

$$W = mg$$

$$F = ma$$

$$E_w = Fd$$

$$E_h = ml$$

Additional Relationships

Circle

circumference = $2\pi r$

area = πr^2

Sphere

area = $4\pi r^2$

volume = $\frac{4}{3}\pi r^3$

Trigonometry

$\sin \theta = \dfrac{\text{opposite}}{\text{hypotenuse}}$

$\cos \theta = \dfrac{\text{adjacent}}{\text{hypotenuse}}$

$\tan \theta = \dfrac{\text{opposite}}{\text{adjacent}}$

$\sin^2 \theta + \cos^2 \theta = 1$

Electron Arrangements of Elements

Group 1	Group 2												Group 3	Group 4	Group 5	Group 6	Group 7	Group 0
(1)	(2)												(13)	(14)	(15)	(16)	(17)	(18)
1 **H** Hydrogen 1																		2 **He** Helium 2
3 **Li** Lithium 2,1	4 **Be** Beryllium 2,2												5 **B** Boron 2,3	6 **C** Carbon 2,4	7 **N** Nitrogen 2,5	8 **O** Oxygen 2,6	9 **F** Fluorine 2,7	10 **Ne** Neon 2,8
11 **Na** Sodium 2,8,1	12 **Mg** Magnesium 2,8,2	(3)	(4)	(5)	(6)	(7)	(8)	(9)	(10)	(11)	(12)	Transition Elements	13 **Al** Aluminium 2,8,3	14 **Si** Silicon 2,8,4	15 **P** Phosphorus 2,8,5	16 **S** Sulfur 2,8,6	17 **Cl** Chlorine 2,8,7	18 **Ar** Argon 2,8,8
19 **K** Potassium 2,8,8,1	20 **Ca** Calcium 2,8,8,2	21 **Sc** Scandium 2,8,9,2	22 **Ti** Titanium 2,8,10,2	23 **V** Vanadium 2,8,11,2	24 **Cr** Chromium 2,8,13,1	25 **Mn** Manganese 2,8,13,2	26 **Fe** Iron 2,8,14,2	27 **Co** Cobalt 2,8,15,2	28 **Ni** Nickel 2,8,16,2	29 **Cu** Copper 2,8,18,1	30 **Zn** Zinc 2,8,18,2		31 **Ga** Gallium 2,8,18,3	32 **Ge** Germanium 2,8,18,4	33 **As** Arsenic 2,8,18,5	34 **Se** Selenium 2,8,18,6	35 **Br** Bromine 2,8,18,7	36 **Kr** Krypton 2,8,18,8
37 **Rb** Rubidium 2,8,18,8,1	38 **Sr** Strontium 2,8,18,8,2	39 **Y** Yttrium 2,8,18,9,2	40 **Zr** Zirconium 2,8,18,10,2	41 **Nb** Niobium 2,8,18,12,1	42 **Mo** Molybdenum 2,8,18,13,1	43 **Tc** Technetium 2,8,18,13,2	44 **Ru** Ruthenium 2,8,18,15,1	45 **Rh** Rhodium 2,8,18,16,1	46 **Pd** Palladium 2,8,18,18,0	47 **Ag** Silver 2,8,18,18,1	48 **Cd** Cadmium 2,8,18,18,2		49 **In** Indium 2,8,18,18,3	50 **Sn** Tin 2,8,18,18,4	51 **Sb** Antimony 2,8,18,18,5	52 **Te** Tellurium 2,8,18,18,6	53 **I** Iodine 2,8,18,18,7	54 **Xe** Xenon 2,8,18,18,8
55 **Cs** Caesium 2,8,18,18,8,1	56 **Ba** Barium 2,8,18,18,8,2	57 **La** Lanthanum 2,8,18,18,9,2	72 **Hf** Hafnium 2,8,18,32,10,2	73 **Ta** Tantalum 2,8,18,32,11,2	74 **W** Tungsten 2,8,18,32,12,2	75 **Re** Rhenium 2,8,18,32,13,2	76 **Os** Osmium 2,8,18,32,14,2	77 **Ir** Iridium 2,8,18,32,15,2	78 **Pt** Platinum 2,8,18,32,17,1	79 **Au** Gold 2,8,18,32,18,1	80 **Hg** Mercury 2,8,18,32,18,2		81 **Tl** Thallium 2,8,18,32,18,3	82 **Pb** Lead 2,8,18,32,18,4	83 **Bi** Bismuth 2,8,18,32,18,5	84 **Po** Polonium 2,8,18,32,18,6	85 **At** Astatine 2,8,18,32,18,7	86 **Rn** Radon 2,8,18,32,18,8
87 **Fr** Francium 2,8,18,32,18,8,1	88 **Ra** Radium 2,8,18,32,18,8,2	89 **Ac** Actinium 2,8,18,32,18,9,2	104 **Rf** Rutherfordium 2,8,18,32,32,10,2	105 **Db** Dubnium 2,8,18,32,32,11,2	106 **Sg** Seaborgium 2,8,18,32,32,12,2	107 **Bh** Bohrium 2,8,18,32,32,13,2	108 **Hs** Hassium 2,8,18,32,32,14,2	109 **Mt** Meitnerium 2,8,18,32,32,15,2	110 **Ds** Darmstadtium 2,8,18,32,32,17,1	111 **Rg** Roentgenium 2,8,18,32,32,18,1	112 **Cn** Copernicium 2,8,18,32,32,18,2							

Key
Atomic number
Symbol
Electron arrangement
Name

Lanthanides

| 57 **La** Lanthanum 2,8,18,18,9,2 | 58 **Ce** Cerium 2,8,18,20,8,2 | 59 **Pr** Praseodymium 2,8,18,21,8,2 | 60 **Nd** Neodymium 2,8,18,22,8,2 | 61 **Pm** Promethium 2,8,18,23,8,2 | 62 **Sm** Samarium 2,8,18,24,8,2 | 63 **Eu** Europium 2,8,18,25,8,2 | 64 **Gd** Gadolinium 2,8,18,25,9,2 | 65 **Tb** Terbium 2,8,18,27,8,2 | 66 **Dy** Dysprosium 2,8,18,28,8,2 | 67 **Ho** Holmium 2,8,18,29,8,2 | 68 **Er** Erbium 2,8,18,30,8,2 | 69 **Tm** Thulium 2,8,18,31,8,2 | 70 **Yb** Ytterbium 2,8,18,32,8,2 | 71 **Lu** Lutetium 2,8,18,32,9,2 |

Actinides

| 89 **Ac** Actinium 2,8,18,32,18,9,2 | 90 **Th** Thorium 2,8,18,32,18,10,2 | 91 **Pa** Protactinium 2,8,18,32,20,9,2 | 92 **U** Uranium 2,8,18,32,21,9,2 | 93 **Np** Neptunium 2,8,18,32,22,9,2 | 94 **Pu** Plutonium 2,8,18,32,24,8,2 | 95 **Am** Americium 2,8,18,32,25,8,2 | 96 **Cm** Curium 2,8,18,32,25,9,2 | 97 **Bk** Berkelium 2,8,18,32,27,8,2 | 98 **Cf** Californium 2,8,18,32,28,8,2 | 99 **Es** Einsteinium 2,8,18,32,29,8,2 | 100 **Fm** Fermium 2,8,18,32,30,8,2 | 101 **Md** Mendelevium 2,8,18,32,31,8,2 | 102 **No** Nobelium 2,8,18,32,32,8,2 | 103 **Lr** Lawrencium 2,8,18,32,32,9,2 |

National Qualifications 2017

Mark

X757/75/01

**Physics
Section 1—Answer Grid
And Section 2**

WEDNESDAY, 17 MAY
1:00 PM – 3:00 PM

Fill in these boxes and read what is printed below.

Full name of centre

Town

Forename(s)

Surname

Number of seat

Date of birth
Day   Month   Year

Scottish candidate number

Total marks — 110

SECTION 1 — 20 marks
Attempt ALL questions.
Instructions for completion of Section 1 are given on *Page two*.

SECTION 2 — 90 marks
Attempt ALL questions.

Reference may be made to the Data Sheet on *Page two* of the question paper X757/75/02 and to the Relationship Sheet X757/75/11.

Write your answers clearly in the spaces provided in this booklet. Additional space for answers and rough work is provided at the end of this booklet. If you use this space you must clearly identify the question number you are attempting. Any rough work must be written in this booklet. You should score through your rough work when you have written your final copy.

Use **blue** or **black** ink.

Before leaving the examination room you must give this booklet to the Invigilator; if you do not, you may lose all the marks for this paper.

SECTION 1 — 20 marks

The questions for Section 1 are contained in the question paper X757/75/02.

Read these and record your answers on the answer grid on *Page three* opposite.

Use blue or black ink. Do NOT use gel pens or pencil.

1. The answer to each question is **either** A, B, C, D or E. Decide what your answer is, then fill in the appropriate bubble (see sample question below).

2. There is **only one correct** answer to each question.

3. Any rough work must be written in the additional space for answers and rough work at the end of this booklet.

Sample Question

The energy unit measured by the electricity meter in your home is the:

    A   ampere

    B   kilowatt-hour

    C   watt

    D   coulomb

    E   volt.

The correct answer is **B** — kilowatt-hour. The answer **B** bubble has been clearly filled in (see below).

Changing an answer

If you decide to change your answer, cancel your first answer by putting a cross through it (see below) and fill in the answer you want. The answer below has been changed to **D**.

If you then decide to change back to an answer you have already scored out, put a tick (✓) to the **right** of the answer you want, as shown below:

SECTION 1 — Answer Grid

	A	B	C	D	E
1	○	○	○	○	○
2	○	○	○	○	○
3	○	○	○	○	○
4	○	○	○	○	○
5	○	○	○	○	○
6	○	○	○	○	○
7	○	○	○	○	○
8	○	○	○	○	○
9	○	○	○	○	○
10	○	○	○	○	○
11	○	○	○	○	○
12	○	○	○	○	○
13	○	○	○	○	○
14	○	○	○	○	○
15	○	○	○	○	○
16	○	○	○	○	○
17	○	○	○	○	○
18	○	○	○	○	○
19	○	○	○	○	○
20	○	○	○	○	○

[Turn over

[BLANK PAGE]

DO NOT WRITE ON THIS PAGE

[TURN OVER FOR NEXT QUESTION]

DO NOT WRITE ON THIS PAGE

SECTION 2 — 90 marks

Attempt ALL questions

1. The rating plate on a food blender is shown.

   Model: FB67P
   230 V a.c.   50 Hz
   290 W

   (a) The plugs on all modern electrical appliances in the UK are fitted with fuses rated at either 3A or 13A.

   (i) Draw the circuit symbol for a fuse. **1**

   (ii) State the purpose of the fuse fitted in the plug of an appliance. **1**

   (iii) Determine the rating of the fuse fitted in the plug of the blender. Justify your answer by calculation. **4**
   Space for working and answer

1. (continued)

   (b) The blender is connected to an alternating current (a.c.) supply.
   Explain in terms of electron flow what is meant by *alternating current*. **1**

2. A student sets up the following circuit.

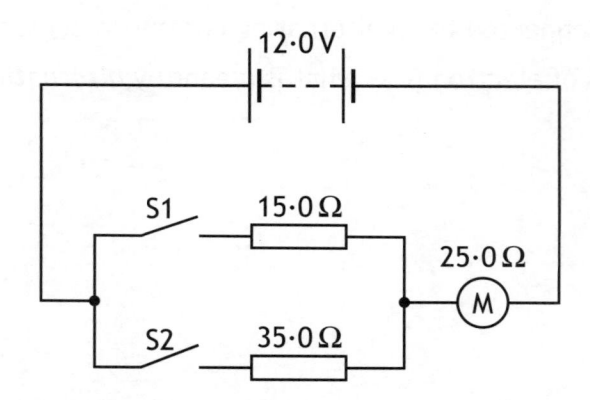

(a) The student closes switch S1.

   (i) Calculate the voltage across the motor.

   Space for working and answer

   (ii) Calculate the power dissipated in the motor.

   Space for working and answer

2. (continued)

(b) The student now also closes switch S2.

(i) Calculate the combined resistance of the two resistors. **3**

Space for working and answer

(ii) State the effect that closing switch S2 has on the power dissipated in the motor.

Justify your answer. **3**

3. A bicycle pump with a sealed outlet contains $4.0 \times 10^{-4}\,m^3$ of air.

   The air inside the pump is at an initial pressure of $1.0 \times 10^5\,Pa$.

   The piston of the pump is now pushed slowly inwards until the volume of air in the pump is $1.6 \times 10^{-4}\,m^3$ as shown.

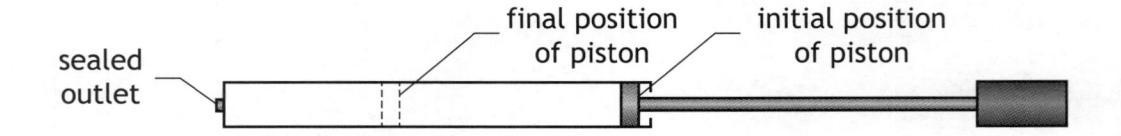

   During this time the temperature of the air in the pump remains constant.

   (a) Calculate the final pressure of the air inside the pump. **3**

   Space for working and answer

   (b) Using the kinetic model, explain what happens to the pressure of the air inside the pump as its volume decreases. **3**

3. (continued)

(c) The piston is now released, allowing it to move outwards towards its original position.

During this time the temperature of the air in the pump remains constant.

Using the axes provided, sketch a graph to show how the pressure of the air in the pump varies as its volume increases.

Numerical values are not required on either axis. **2**

(An additional diagram, if required, can be found on *Page twenty-eight*)

4. A student observes water waves entering a harbour.

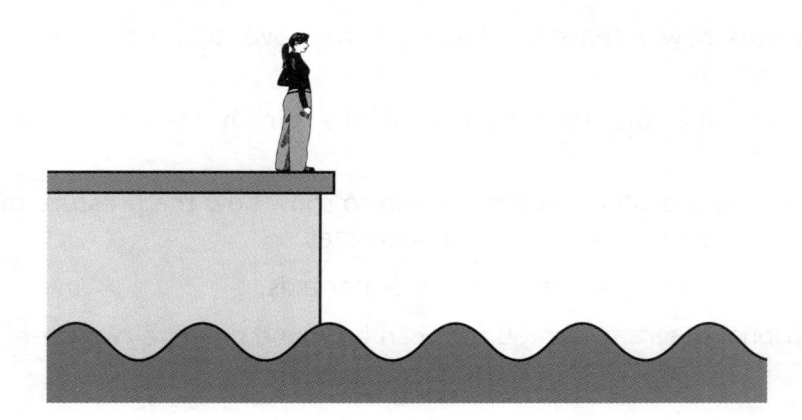

(a) To determine the frequency of the waves, the student measures the time taken for a wave to pass a point at the harbour entrance.

The student measures this time to be 2·5 s

(i) Calculate the frequency of the waves.

Space for working and answer

(ii) Suggest how the accuracy of the frequency determined by the student could be improved.

4. (continued)

(b) The distance between one wave crest and the next crest is 8·0 m.

Calculate the velocity of the waves. **3**

Space for working and answer

(c) Waves travel towards the entrance of the harbour as shown.

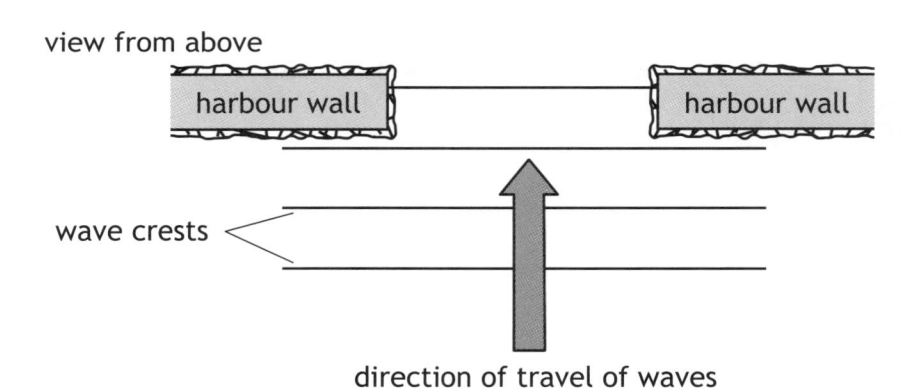

view from above

harbour wall   harbour wall

wave crests

direction of travel of waves

Complete the diagram to show the pattern of wave crests inside the harbour. **2**

(An additional diagram, if required, can be found on *Page twenty-eight*)

(d) As the waves pass into the harbour the student observes that the amplitude of the waves decreases.

Explain this observation. **1**

5. Alpha, beta and gamma are types of nuclear radiation, which have a range of properties and effects.

Using your knowledge of physics, comment on the similarities and/or differences between these types of nuclear radiation.

3

6. A technician uses the apparatus shown to investigate the effect of shielding gamma radiation with lead.

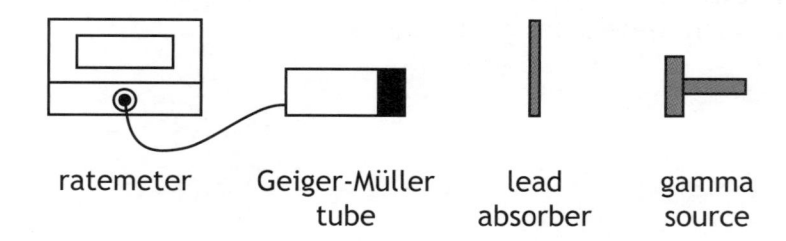

Gamma radiation passing through a lead absorber is detected by a Geiger-Müller tube. The count rate is displayed on the ratemeter.

The count rates for a range of different thicknesses of lead absorber are recorded.

Using these results the technician produces a graph of corrected count rate against thickness of lead absorber as shown.

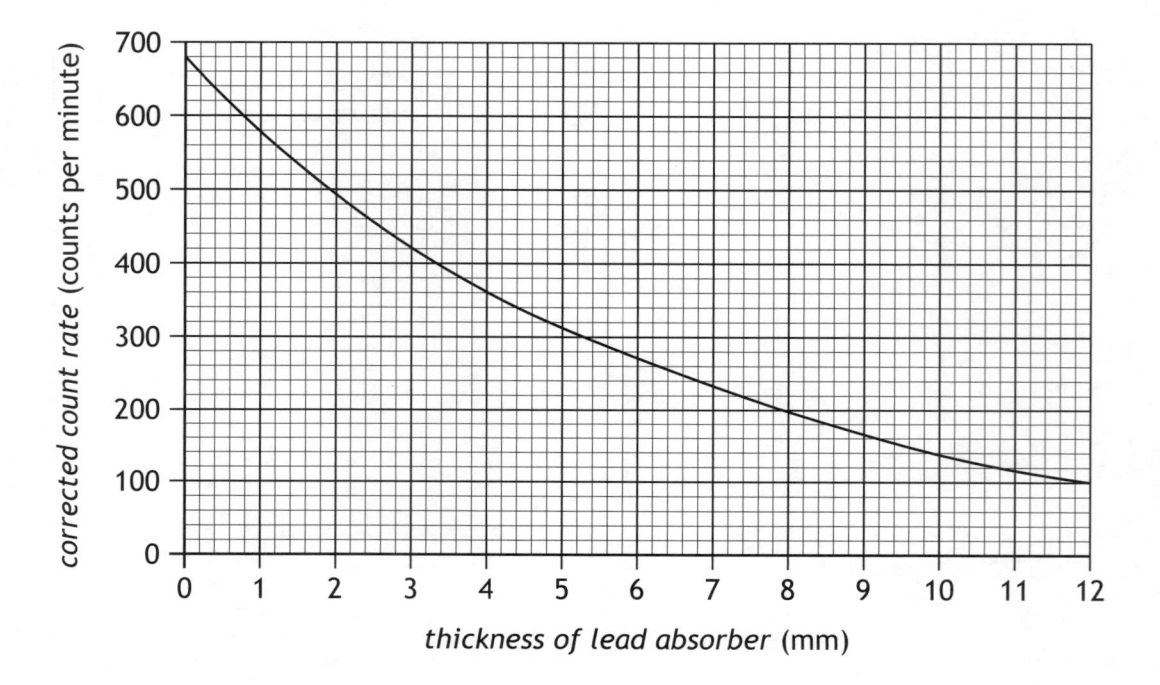

(a) State what additional measurement the technician must have made in order to determine the corrected count rate. **1**

6. (continued)

   (b) The half-value thickness of a material is the thickness of material required to reduce the corrected count rate from a source by half.

   (i) Using the graph, determine the half-value thickness of lead for this source of gamma radiation.

   (ii) Determine the thickness of lead required to reduce the corrected count rate to one eighth of its initial value.

   Space for working and answer

   (iii) The technician suggests repeating the experiment with aluminium absorbers instead of lead absorbers.

   Predict how the half-value thickness of aluminium would compare to the half-value thickness of lead for this source.

   (c) When working with the radioactive source the technician is exposed to an equivalent dose rate of $2·5 \times 10^{-6}$ Sv h^{-1}.

   The annual equivalent dose limit for the technician is 20 mSv.

   Calculate the maximum number of hours the technician may work with this source without exceeding this limit.

   Space for working and answer

7. Nuclear reactions are used to generate electrical energy in a nuclear power station.

   (a) The fuel for the power station is in the form of pellets, containing uranium-235.

   A fuel pellet has an activity of 80 kBq.

   State what is meant by an *activity of 80 kBq*. **1**

   (b) In a nuclear reaction a uranium-235 nucleus is split by a neutron to produce two smaller nuclei, three neutrons, and energy.

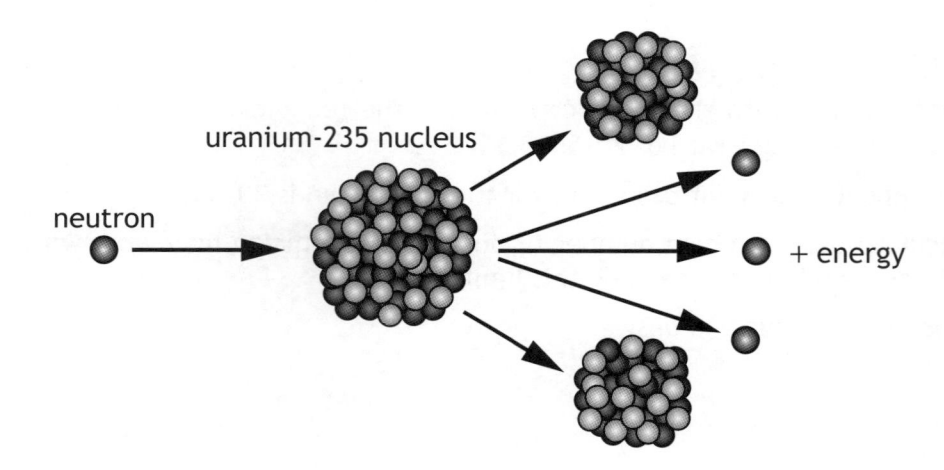

7. (b) (continued)

(i) Explain how a single reaction can lead to the continuous generation of energy. **2**

(ii) One nuclear reaction releases 3.2×10^{-11} J.

In the reactor, 3.0×10^{21} reactions occur each minute.

Determine the maximum power output of the reactor. **4**

Space for working and answer

(c) The nuclear reactor produces waste that emits nuclear radiation.

State a use of nuclear radiation. **1**

8. In speedway, motorbikes are raced anticlockwise round an oval track.

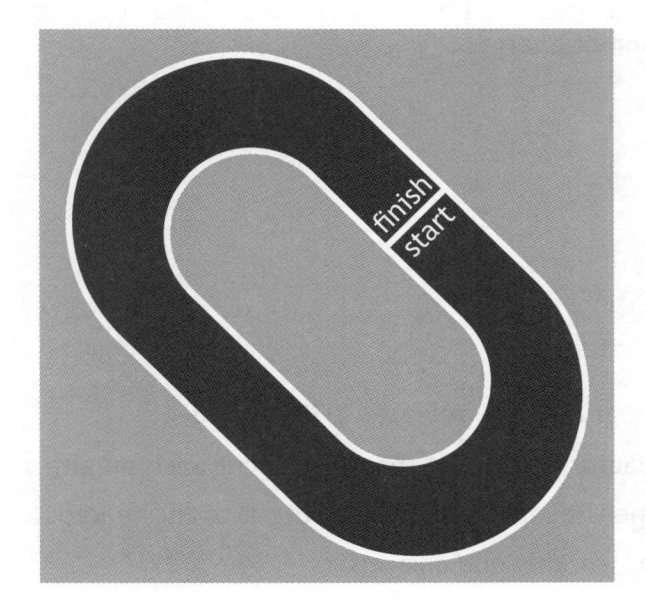

   A race consists of four laps of a 380 m track.

   (a) State the displacement of a motorbike from the start line to the finish line for a complete race. **1**

   (b) The speed-time graph of a motorbike for the first 8·0 s of a race is shown.

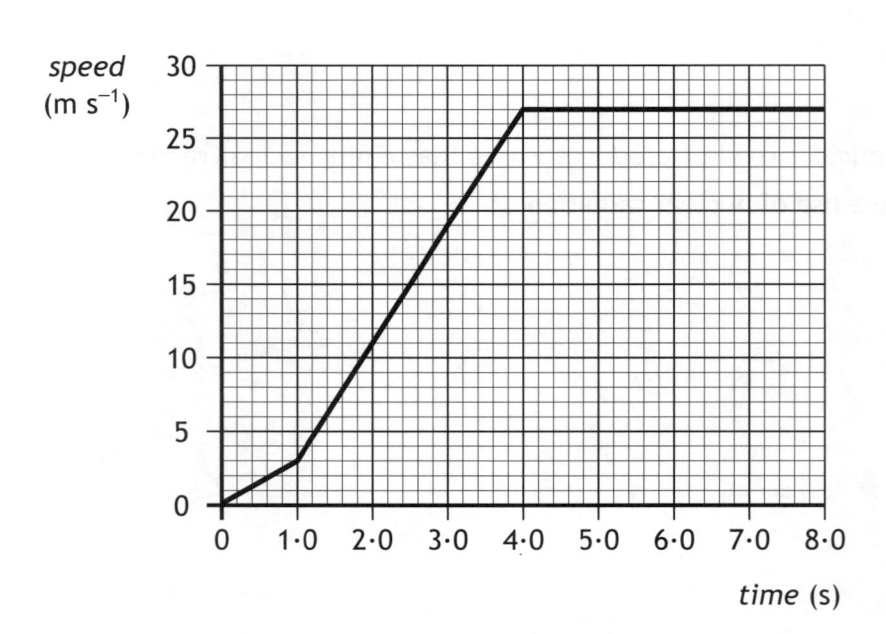

8. (b) (continued)

(i) Calculate the distance travelled by the motorbike in the first 4·0 s of the race.

Space for working and answer

(ii) Determine the **greatest** acceleration of the motorbike during the first 8·0 s of the race.

Space for working and answer

(c) The winner of the race completes all four laps in a time of 79 s.

Calculate the average speed of the winner.

Space for working and answer

9. A weightlifter applies an upwards force of 1176 N to a barbell to hold it in a stationary position as shown.

(a) Describe how the upward force exerted by the weightlifter on the barbell compares to the weight of the barbell.

(b) Calculate the mass of the barbell.

Space for working and answer

(c) The weightlifter increases the upward force on the barbell to 1344 N in order to lift the barbell above their head.

Calculate the initial acceleration of the barbell.

Space for working and answer

10. An articulated lorry has six pairs of wheels.

One pair of wheels can be raised off the ground.

Using your knowledge of physics, comment on situations in which the wheels may be raised or lowered. 3

11. A tennis player serves a tennis ball horizontally at a velocity of 42 m s^{-1}.

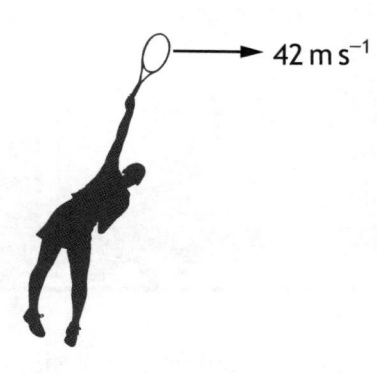

→ 42 m s^{-1}

The effects of air resistance are negligible.

(a) State which of the following graphs P, Q or R shows the vertical velocity of the ball after it leaves the player's racquet.

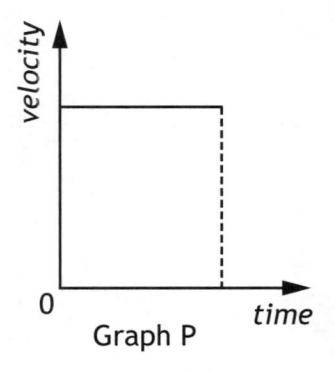

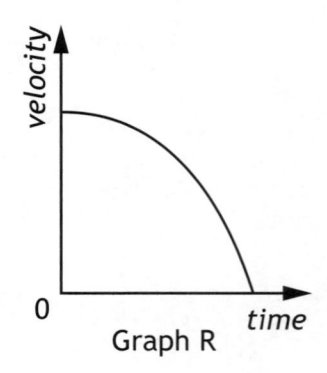

Graph P: velocity constant vs time
Graph Q: velocity increasing linearly from 0 vs time
Graph R: velocity decreasing curve vs time

Graph: _____

(b) In a second serve the player hits the ball horizontally with a smaller velocity from the same height.

State whether the time taken for the ball to reach the ground is less than, equal to, or greater than the time taken in the first serve.

Justify your answer.

11. (continued)

(c) The tennis court has a retractable roof to allow play to continue in all weather conditions.

It requires 5·5 kJ of energy to move one section of the roof a distance of 25 m.

Calculate the average force acting on this section of the roof while it is being moved.

Space for working and answer

[Turn over for next question

12. The star Wolf 359 is at a distance of 7·8 light-years from Earth.

A radio signal from Wolf 359 is detected by a radio telescope on Earth.

(a) (i) State the speed of the radio waves.

(ii) Calculate the distance, in metres, from Wolf 359 to Earth.

Space for working and answer

(b) Another telescope is used to observe the same star in the visible part of the spectrum.

(i) State a suitable detector of visible light that may be used in this telescope.

(ii) State whether the time taken for the visible light from the star to reach Earth is less than, equal to, or greater than the time taken for the radio waves from the star to reach Earth.

[END OF QUESTION PAPER]

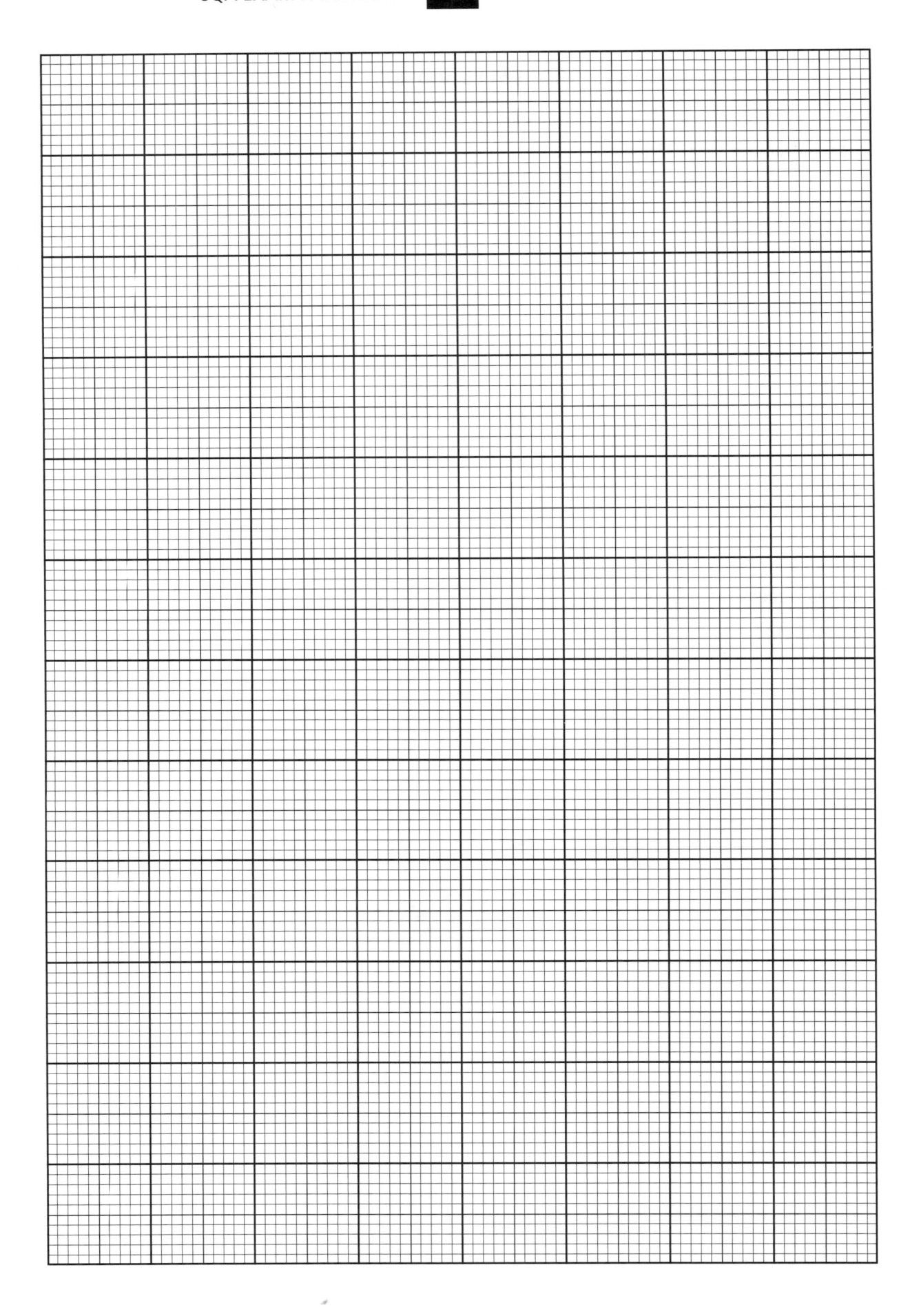

ADDITIONAL SPACE FOR ANSWERS AND ROUGH WORKING

Additional diagram for Q3 (c)

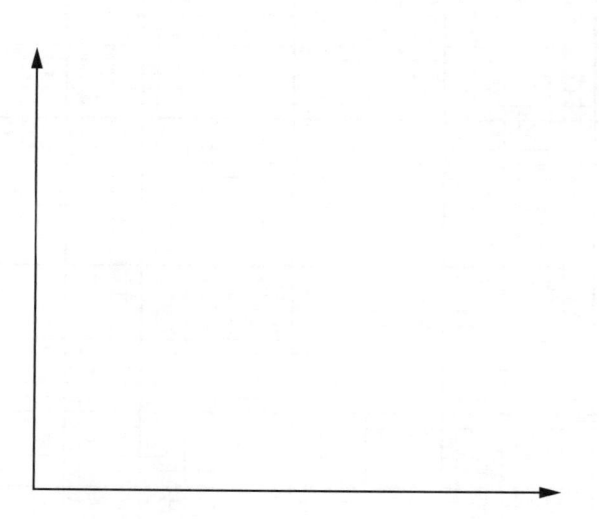

Additional diagram for Q4 (c)

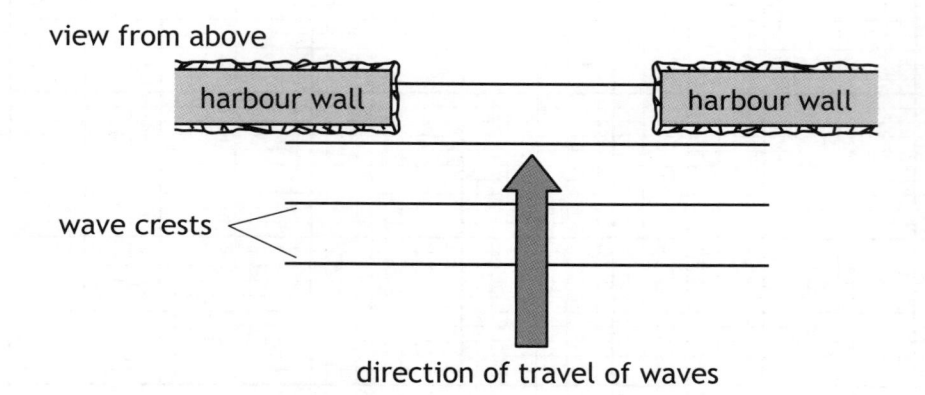

view from above

harbour wall   harbour wall

wave crests

direction of travel of waves

ADDITIONAL SPACE FOR ANSWERS AND ROUGH WORKING

[Turn over

ADDITIONAL SPACE FOR ANSWERS AND ROUGH WORKING

NATIONAL 5
2017 Specimen Question Paper

N5

National Qualifications
SPECIMEN ONLY

S857/75/02

Physics
Section 1—Questions

Date — Not applicable

Duration — 2 hours 30 minutes

Instructions for completion of Section 1 are given on *Page two* of your question and answer booklet S857/75/01.

Record your answers on the answer grid on *Page three* of your question and answer booklet.

Reference may be made to the Data Sheet on *Page two* of this booklet and to the Relationships Sheet S857/75/11.

Before leaving the examination room you must give your question and answer booklet to the Invigilator; if you do not, you may lose all the marks for this paper.

SQA

DATA SHEET

Speed of light in materials

Material	Speed in m s^{-1}
Air	3.0×10^8
Carbon dioxide	3.0×10^8
Diamond	1.2×10^8
Glass	2.0×10^8
Glycerol	2.1×10^8
Water	2.3×10^8

Speed of sound in materials

Material	Speed in m s^{-1}
Aluminium	5200
Air	340
Bone	4100
Carbon dioxide	270
Glycerol	1900
Muscle	1600
Steel	5200
Tissue	1500
Water	1500

Gravitational field strengths

	Gravitational field strength on the surface in N kg^{-1}
Earth	9.8
Jupiter	23
Mars	3.7
Mercury	3.7
Moon	1.6
Neptune	11
Saturn	9.0
Sun	270
Uranus	8.7
Venus	8.9

Specific heat capacity of materials

Material	Specific heat capacity in J kg^{-1} °C^{-1}
Alcohol	2350
Aluminium	902
Copper	386
Glass	500
Ice	2100
Iron	480
Lead	128
Oil	2130
Water	4180

Specific latent heat of fusion of materials

Material	Specific latent heat of fusion in J kg^{-1}
Alcohol	0.99×10^5
Aluminium	3.95×10^5
Carbon Dioxide	1.80×10^5
Copper	2.05×10^5
Iron	2.67×10^5
Lead	0.25×10^5
Water	3.34×10^5

Melting and boiling points of materials

Material	Melting point in °C	Boiling point in °C
Alcohol	−98	65
Aluminium	660	2470
Copper	1077	2567
Glycerol	18	290
Lead	328	1737
Iron	1537	2737

Specific latent heat of vaporisation of materials

Material	Specific latent heat of vaporisation in J kg^{-1}
Alcohol	11.2×10^5
Carbon Dioxide	3.77×10^5
Glycerol	8.30×10^5
Turpentine	2.90×10^5
Water	22.6×10^5

Radiation weighting factors

Type of radiation	Radiation weighting factor
alpha	20
beta	1
fast neutrons	10
gamma	1
slow neutrons	3
X-rays	1

SECTION 1

Attempt ALL questions

1. Which of the following contains two scalar quantities?

    A   Force and mass
    B   Weight and mass
    C   Displacement and speed
    D   Distance and speed
    E   Displacement and velocity

2. A student sets up the apparatus as shown.

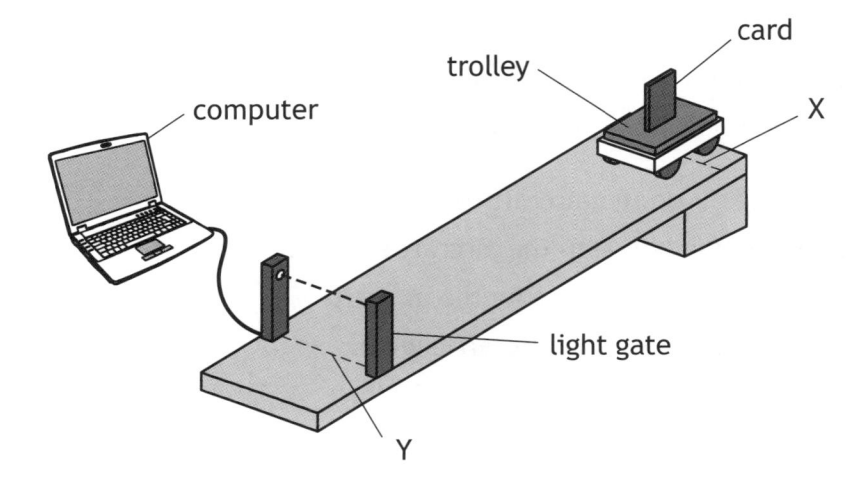

    The trolley is released from X and moves down the ramp.
    The following measurements are recorded.

    time for card to pass through light gate = 0·080 s
    distance from X to Y = 0·50 m
    length of card = 0·040 m

    The instantaneous speed of the trolley at Y is

    A   0·50 m s^{-1}
    B   1·6 m s^{-1}
    C   2·0 m s^{-1}
    D   3·2 m s^{-1}
    E   6·3 m s^{-1}.

[Turn over

3. A block of mass 3 kg is pulled across a horizontal bench by a force of 20 N as shown below.

   20 N ← [3 kg]

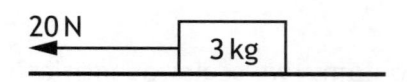

   The block accelerates at $4\,m\,s^{-2}$.

   The force of friction between the block and the bench is

   A   0 N
   B   8 N
   C   12 N
   D   20 N
   E   32 N.

4. An aircraft engine exerts a force on the air.

   Which of the following completes the 'Newton pair' of forces?

   A   The force of the air on the aircraft engine.
   B   The force of friction between the aircraft engine and the air.
   C   The force of the aircraft engine on the aircraft.
   D   The force of the Earth on the aircraft engine.
   E   The force of the aircraft engine on the Earth.

5. A trolley of mass 0·50 kg has a kinetic energy of 0·36 J.

   The speed of the trolley is

   A $0\cdot60\,m\,s^{-1}$
   B $0\cdot85\,m\,s^{-1}$
   C $1\cdot2\,m\,s^{-1}$
   D $1\cdot44\,m\,s^{-1}$
   E $1\cdot7\,m\,s^{-1}$.

6. A ball is released from rest and allowed to roll down a curved track as shown.

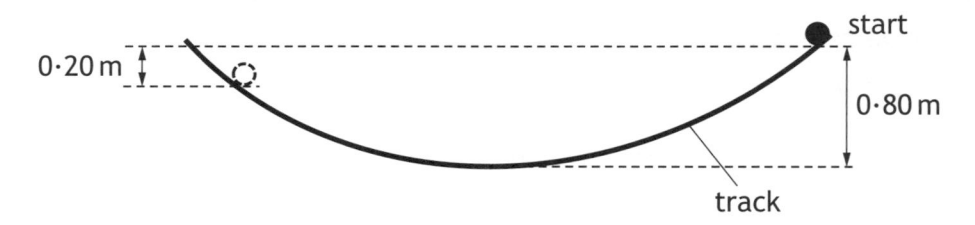

The mass of the ball is 0·50 kg.

The maximum height reached on the opposite side of the track is 0·20 m lower than the height of the starting point.

The amount of energy lost is

A   0·080 J
B   0·10 J
C   0·98 J
D   2·9 J
E   3·9 J.

7. The Mars Curiosity Rover has a mass of 900 kg.

Which row of the table gives the mass and weight of the Rover on Mars?

	Mass (kg)	Weight (N)
A	243	243
B	243	900
C	900	900
D	900	3330
E	900	8820

8. A student makes the following statements about the Universe.

   I   The Big Bang Theory is a theory about the origin of the Universe.
   II The Universe is approximately 14 million years old.
   III The Universe is expanding.

   Which of these statements is/are correct?

   A   I only
   B   II only
   C   I and II only
   D   I and III only
   E   I, II and III

9. A conductor carries a current of 4·0 µA for 250 s.

   The total charge passing a point in the conductor is

   A $1·6 \times 10^{-8}$ C
   B $1·0 \times 10^{-3}$ C
   C $6·25 \times 10^{1}$ C
   D $1·0 \times 10^{3}$ C
   E $6·25 \times 10^{7}$ C.

10. A uniform electric field exists between plates Q and R.

    The diagram shows the path taken by a particle as it passes through the field.

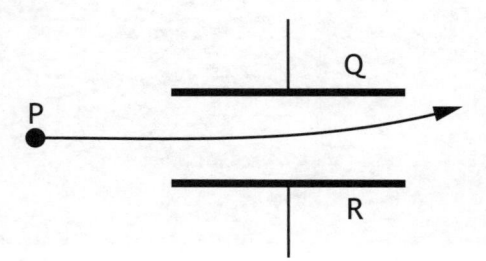

    Which row in the table identifies the charge on the particle, the charge on plate Q and the charge on plate R?

	Charge on particle	Charge on plate Q	Charge on plate R
A	negative	positive	negative
B	negative	negative	positive
C	no charge	negative	positive
D	no charge	positive	negative
E	positive	positive	negative

11. 1 volt is equivalent to

    A 1 ampere per watt
    B 1 coulomb per second
    C 1 joule per coulomb
    D 1 joule per second
    E 1 watt per second.

12. In the circuit shown, the current in each resistor is different.

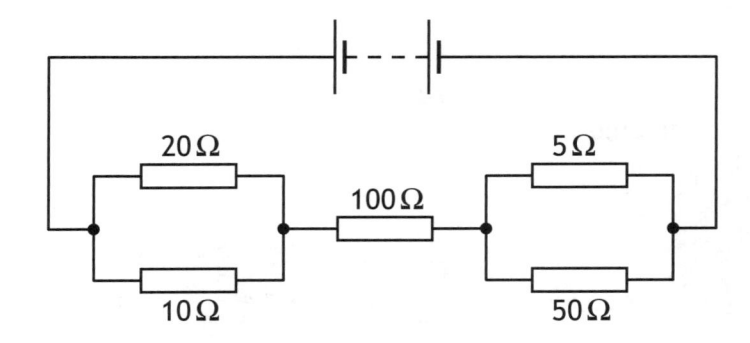

    In which resistor is the current smallest?

    A 5 Ω
    B 10 Ω
    C 20 Ω
    D 50 Ω
    E 100 Ω

13. Five students each carry out an experiment to determine the specific heat capacity of copper. The setup used by each student is shown.

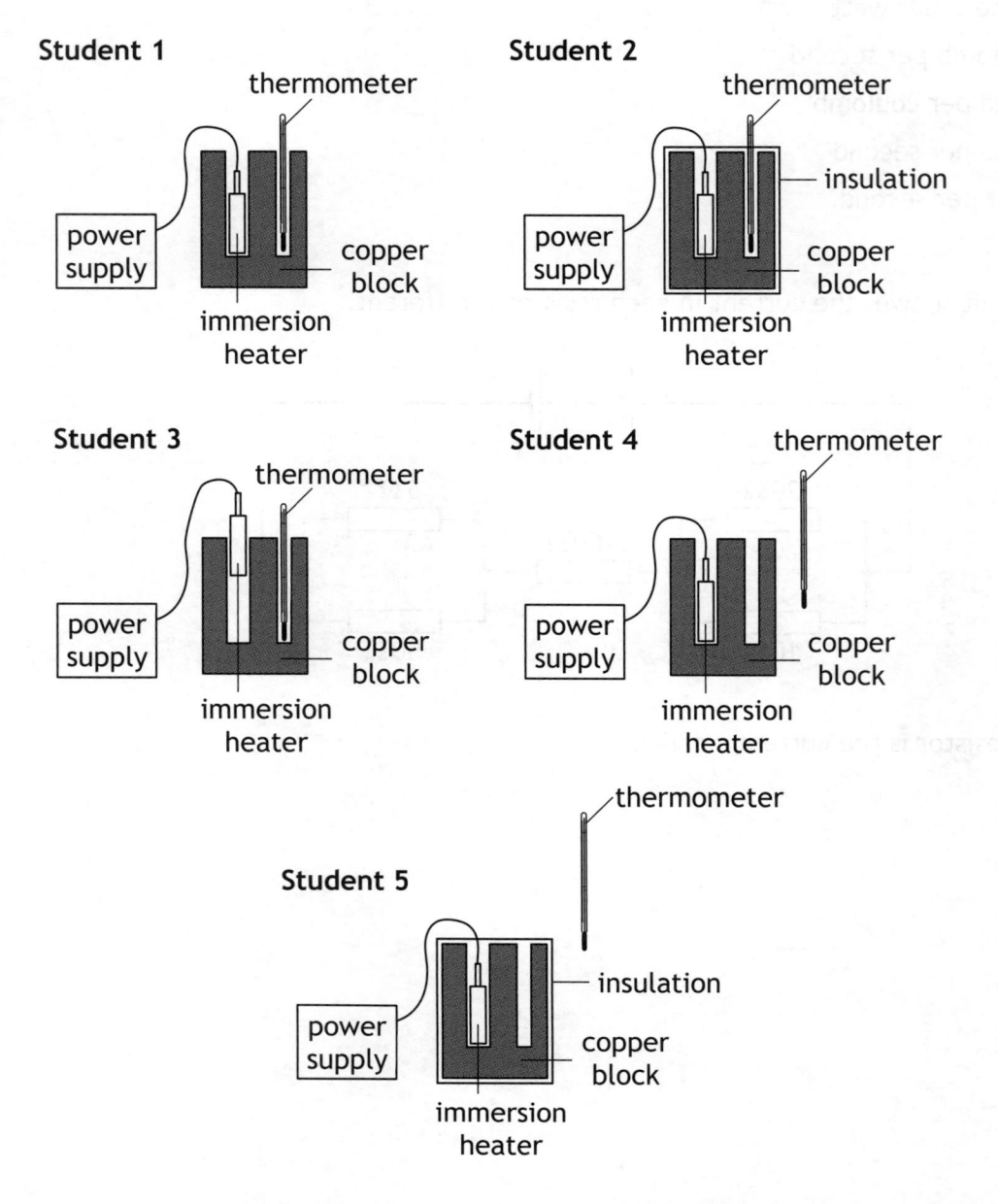

Student 1

Student 2

Student 3

Student 4

Student 5

The student with the setup that would allow the most accurate value for the specific heat capacity of copper to be determined is

A student 1
B student 2
C student 3
D student 4
E student 5.

[Turn over

14. Three resistors are connected as shown.

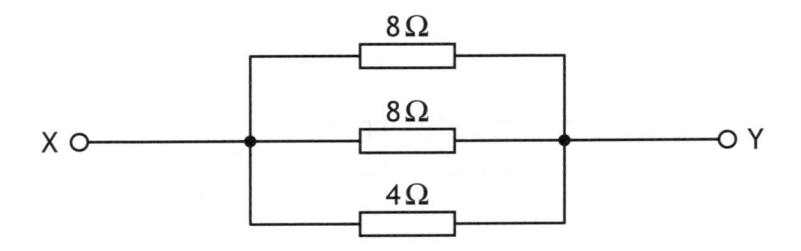

The resistance between X and Y is

A 0·08 Ω
B 0·5 Ω
C 2 Ω
D 13 Ω
E 20 Ω.

15. A heater is immersed in a substance.

The heater is then switched on.

The graph shows the temperature of the substance over a period of time.

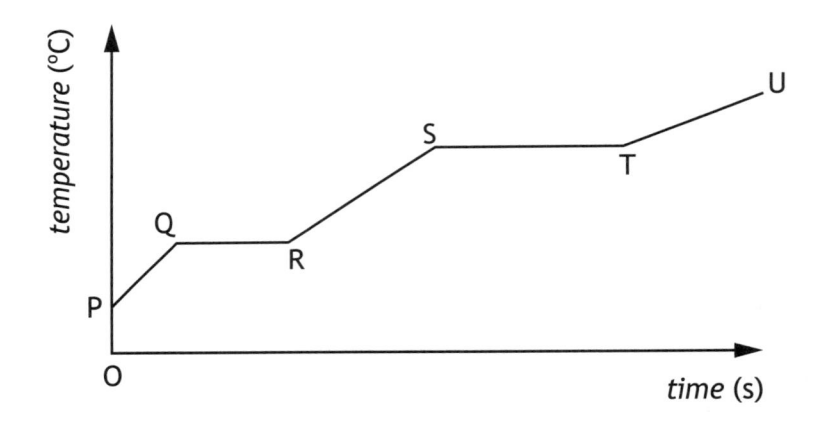

Which row in the table identifies the sections of the graph when the substance is changing state?

	Solid to liquid	Liquid to gas
A	QR	TU
B	QR	ST
C	PQ	RS
D	PQ	TU
E	ST	QR

16. A bicycle pump is sealed at one end and the piston pushed until the pressure of the trapped air is 4.00×10^5 Pa.

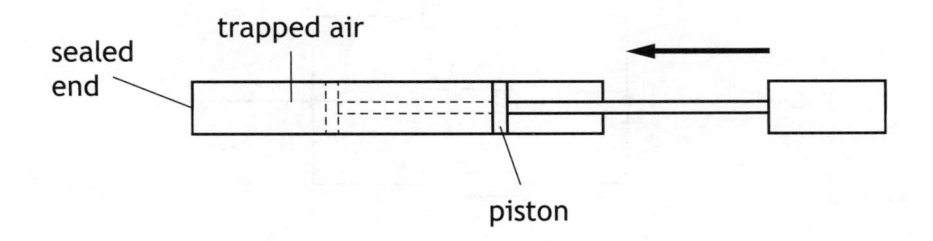

The area of the piston compressing the air is 5.00×10^{-4} m².

The force that the trapped air exerts on the piston is

- A 1.25×10^{-9} N
- B 8.00×10^{-1} N
- C 2.00×10^{2} N
- D 8.00×10^{8} N
- E 2.00×10^{10} N.

17. A liquid is heated from 17 °C to 50 °C. The temperature rise in kelvin is

- A 33 K
- B 67 K
- C 306 K
- D 340 K
- E 579 K.

[Turn over

18. The following diagram shows a wave.

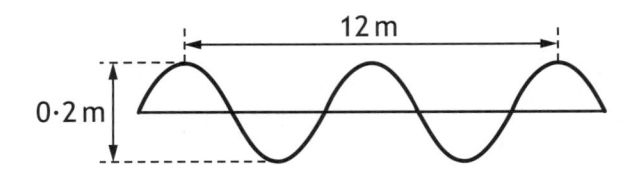

Which row in the table gives the wavelength and amplitude of the wave?

	Wavelength (m)	Amplitude (m)
A	4	0·2
B	6	0·1
C	6	0·2
D	12	0·1
E	12	0·2

19. A wave machine in a swimming pool generates 15 waves per minute.

The wavelength of these waves is 2·0 m.

The frequency of the waves is

A   0·25 Hz
B   0·50 Hz
C   4·0 Hz
D   15 Hz
E   30 Hz.

[Turn over

20. The diagram shows members of the electromagnetic spectrum in order of increasing wavelength.

| Gamma rays | P | Ultraviolet radiation | Q | Infrared radiation | R | TV and radio waves |

──────── increasing wavelength ────────▶

Which row in the table identifies the radiations represented by the letters P, Q and R?

	P	Q	R
A	X-rays	visible light	microwaves
B	X-rays	microwaves	visible light
C	microwaves	visible light	X-rays
D	visible light	microwaves	X-rays
E	visible light	X-rays	microwaves

21. A ray of red light is incident on a glass block as shown.

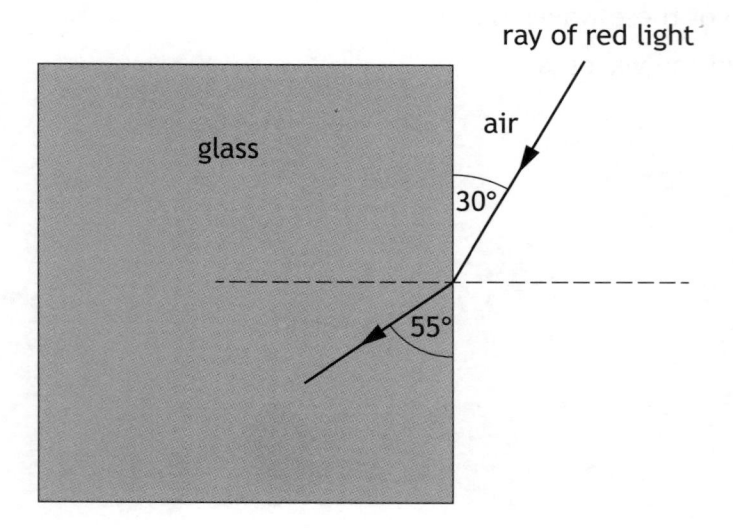

Which row in the table shows the values of the angle of incidence and angle of refraction?

	Angle of incidence	Angle of refraction
A	35°	60°
B	30°	55°
C	30°	35°
D	60°	55°
E	60°	35°

22. Which of the following describes the term ionisation?

    A   An atom losing an orbiting electron.
    B   An atom losing a proton.
    C   A nucleus emitting an alpha particle.
    D   A nucleus emitting a neutron.
    E   A nucleus emitting a gamma ray.

23. A student writes the following statements about the activity of a radioactive source.

    I   The activity decreases with time.
    II   The activity is measured in becquerels.
    III The activity is the number of decays per second.

    Which of these statements is/are correct?

    A   I only
    B   II only
    C   I and II only
    D   II and III only
    E   I, II and III

24. A worker in a nuclear power station is exposed to 3·00 mGy of gamma radiation and 0·500 mGy of fast neutrons.

    The total equivalent dose received by the worker is

    A   3·50 mSv
    B   8·00 mSv
    C   30·5 mSv
    D   35·0 mSv
    E   38·5 mSv.

[Turn over

25. In a nuclear reactor a chain reaction releases energy from nuclei.

Which of the following statements describes the beginning of a chain reaction?

A   An electron splits a nucleus releasing more electrons.

B   An electron splits a nucleus releasing protons.

C   A proton splits a nucleus releasing more protons.

D   A neutron splits a nucleus releasing electrons.

E   A neutron splits a nucleus releasing more neutrons.

[END OF SECTION 1. NOW ATTEMPT THE QUESTIONS IN SECTION 2 OF YOUR QUESTION AND ANSWER BOOKLET]

# S857/75/11

**Physics
Relationships Sheet**

National Qualifications SPECIMEN ONLY

Date — Not applicable
Duration — 2 hours 30 minutes

$$E_p = mgh$$

$$E_k = \tfrac{1}{2}mv^2$$

$$Q = It$$

$$V = IR$$

$$R_T = R_1 + R_2 + \ldots$$

$$\frac{1}{R_T} = \frac{1}{R_1} + \frac{1}{R_2} + \ldots$$

$$V_2 = \left(\frac{R_2}{R_1 + R_2}\right) V_s$$

$$\frac{V_1}{V_2} = \frac{R_1}{R_2}$$

$$P = \frac{E}{t}$$

$$P = IV$$

$$P = I^2 R$$

$$P = \frac{V^2}{R}$$

$$E_h = cm\Delta T$$

$$p = \frac{F}{A}$$

$$\frac{pV}{T} = \text{constant}$$

$$p_1 V_1 = p_2 V_2$$

$$\frac{p_1}{T_1} = \frac{p_2}{T_2}$$

$$\frac{V_1}{T_1} = \frac{V_2}{T_2}$$

$$d = vt$$

$$v = f\lambda$$

$$T = \frac{1}{f}$$

$$A = \frac{N}{t}$$

$$D = \frac{E}{m}$$

$$H = D w_R$$

$$\dot{H} = \frac{H}{t}$$

$$s = vt$$

$$d = \bar{v} t$$

$$s = \bar{v} t$$

$$a = \frac{v - u}{t}$$

$$W = mg$$

$$F = ma$$

$$E_w = Fd$$

$$E_h = ml$$

$$f = \frac{N}{t}$$

Additional Relationships

Circle

circumference = $2\pi r$

area = πr^2

Sphere

area = $4\pi r^2$

volume = $\frac{4}{3}\pi r^3$

Trigonometry

$\sin \theta = \dfrac{\text{opposite}}{\text{hypotenuse}}$

$\cos \theta = \dfrac{\text{adjacent}}{\text{hypotenuse}}$

$\tan \theta = \dfrac{\text{opposite}}{\text{adjacent}}$

$\sin^2 \theta + \cos^2 \theta = 1$

Electron Arrangements of Elements

Group 1	Group 2												Group 3	Group 4	Group 5	Group 6	Group 7	Group 0
(1)	(2)												(13)	(14)	(15)	(16)	(17)	(18)
1 **H** 1 Hydrogen																		2 **He** 2 Helium
3 **Li** 2,1 Lithium	4 **Be** 2,2 Beryllium												5 **B** 2,3 Boron	6 **C** 2,4 Carbon	7 **N** 2,5 Nitrogen	8 **O** 2,6 Oxygen	9 **F** 2,7 Fluorine	10 **Ne** 2,8 Neon
11 **Na** 2,8,1 Sodium	12 **Mg** 2,8,2 Magnesium	(3)	(4)	(5)	(6)	(7)	(8)	(9)	(10)	(11)	(12)	Transition Elements	13 **Al** 2,8,3 Aluminium	14 **Si** 2,8,4 Silicon	15 **P** 2,8,5 Phosphorus	16 **S** 2,8,6 Sulfur	17 **Cl** 2,8,7 Chlorine	18 **Ar** 2,8,8 Argon
19 **K** 2,8,8,1 Potassium	20 **Ca** 2,8,8,2 Calcium	21 **Sc** 2,8,9,2 Scandium	22 **Ti** 2,8,10,2 Titanium	23 **V** 2,8,11,2 Vanadium	24 **Cr** 2,8,13,1 Chromium	25 **Mn** 2,8,13,2 Manganese	26 **Fe** 2,8,14,2 Iron	27 **Co** 2,8,15,2 Cobalt	28 **Ni** 2,8,16,2 Nickel	29 **Cu** 2,8,18,1 Copper	30 **Zn** 2,8,18,2 Zinc		31 **Ga** 2,8,18,3 Gallium	32 **Ge** 2,8,18,4 Germanium	33 **As** 2,8,18,5 Arsenic	34 **Se** 2,8,18,6 Selenium	35 **Br** 2,8,18,7 Bromine	36 **Kr** 2,8,18,8 Krypton
37 **Rb** 2,8,18,8,1 Rubidium	38 **Sr** 2,8,18,8,2 Strontium	39 **Y** 2,8,18,9,2 Yttrium	40 **Zr** 2,8,18,10,2 Zirconium	41 **Nb** 2,8,18,12,1 Niobium	42 **Mo** 2,8,18,13,1 Molybdenum	43 **Tc** 2,8,18,13,2 Technetium	44 **Ru** 2,8,18,15,1 Ruthenium	45 **Rh** 2,8,18,16,1 Rhodium	46 **Pd** 2,8,18,18,0 Palladium	47 **Ag** 2,8,18,18,1 Silver	48 **Cd** 2,8,18,18,2 Cadmium		49 **In** 2,8,18,18,3 Indium	50 **Sn** 2,8,18,18,4 Tin	51 **Sb** 2,8,18,18,5 Antimony	52 **Te** 2,8,18,18,6 Tellurium	53 **I** 2,8,18,18,7 Iodine	54 **Xe** 2,8,18,18,8 Xenon
55 **Cs** 2,8,18,18,8,1 Caesium	56 **Ba** 2,8,18,18,8,2 Barium	57 **La** 2,8,18,18,9,2 Lanthanum	72 **Hf** 2,8,18,32,10,2 Hafnium	73 **Ta** 2,8,18,32,11,2 Tantalum	74 **W** 2,8,18,32,12,2 Tungsten	75 **Re** 2,8,18,32,13,2 Rhenium	76 **Os** 2,8,18,32,14,2 Osmium	77 **Ir** 2,8,18,32,15,2 Iridium	78 **Pt** 2,8,18,32,17,1 Platinum	79 **Au** 2,8,18,32,18,1 Gold	80 **Hg** 2,8,18,32,18,2 Mercury		81 **Tl** 2,8,18,32,18,3 Thallium	82 **Pb** 2,8,18,32,18,4 Lead	83 **Bi** 2,8,18,32,18,5 Bismuth	84 **Po** 2,8,18,32,18,6 Polonium	85 **At** 2,8,18,32,18,7 Astatine	86 **Rn** 2,8,18,32,18,8 Radon
87 **Fr** 2,8,18,32,18,8,1 Francium	88 **Ra** 2,8,18,32,18,8,2 Radium	89 **Ac** 2,8,18,32,18,9,2 Actinium	104 **Rf** 2,8,18,32,32,10,2 Rutherfordium	105 **Db** 2,8,18,32,32,11,2 Dubnium	106 **Sg** 2,8,18,32,32,12,2 Seaborgium	107 **Bh** 2,8,18,32,32,13,2 Bohrium	108 **Hs** 2,8,18,32,32,14,2 Hassium	109 **Mt** 2,8,18,32,32,15,2 Meitnerium	110 **Ds** 2,8,18,32,32,17,1 Darmstadtium	111 **Rg** 2,8,18,32,32,18,1 Roentgenium	112 **Cn** 2,8,18,32,32,18,2 Copernicium							

Key

Atomic number
Symbol
Electron arrangement
Name

Lanthanides

| 57 **La** 2,8,18,18,9,2 Lanthanum | 58 **Ce** 2,8,18,20,8,2 Cerium | 59 **Pr** 2,8,18,21,8,2 Praseodymium | 60 **Nd** 2,8,18,22,8,2 Neodymium | 61 **Pm** 2,8,18,23,8,2 Promethium | 62 **Sm** 2,8,18,24,8,2 Samarium | 63 **Eu** 2,8,18,25,8,2 Europium | 64 **Gd** 2,8,18,25,9,2 Gadolinium | 65 **Tb** 2,8,18,27,8,2 Terbium | 66 **Dy** 2,8,18,28,8,2 Dysprosium | 67 **Ho** 2,8,18,29,8,2 Holmium | 68 **Er** 2,8,18,30,8,2 Erbium | 69 **Tm** 2,8,18,31,8,2 Thulium | 70 **Yb** 2,8,18,32,8,2 Ytterbium | 71 **Lu** 2,8,18,32,9,2 Lutetium |

Actinides

| 89 **Ac** 2,8,18,32,18,9,2 Actinium | 90 **Th** 2,8,18,32,18,10,2 Thorium | 91 **Pa** 2,8,18,32,20,9,2 Protactinium | 92 **U** 2,8,18,32,21,9,2 Uranium | 93 **Np** 2,8,18,32,22,9,2 Neptunium | 94 **Pu** 2,8,18,32,24,8,2 Plutonium | 95 **Am** 2,8,18,32,25,8,2 Americium | 96 **Cm** 2,8,18,32,25,9,2 Curium | 97 **Bk** 2,8,18,32,27,8,2 Berkelium | 98 **Cf** 2,8,18,32,28,8,2 Californium | 99 **Es** 2,8,18,32,29,8,2 Einsteinium | 100 **Fm** 2,8,18,32,30,8,2 Fermium | 101 **Md** 2,8,18,32,31,8,2 Mendelevium | 102 **No** 2,8,18,32,32,8,2 Nobelium | 103 **Lr** 2,8,18,32,32,9,2 Lawrencium |

FOR OFFICIAL USE

N5

National Qualifications
SPECIMEN ONLY

Mark

S857/75/01

Physics
Section 1—Answer Grid
And Section 2

Date — Not applicable

Duration — 2 hours 30 minutes

Fill in these boxes and read what is printed below.

Full name of centre

Town

Forename(s)

Surname

Number of seat

Date of birth

Day   Month   Year   Scottish candidate number

Total marks — 135

SECTION 1 — 25 marks
Attempt ALL questions.
Instructions for completion of Section 1 are given on *Page two*.

SECTION 2 — 110 marks
Attempt ALL questions.

Reference may be made to the Data Sheet on *Page two* of the question paper S857/75/02 and to the Relationships Sheet S857/75/11.

Write your answers clearly in the spaces provided in this booklet. Additional space for answers and rough work is provided at the end of this booklet. If you use this space you must clearly identify the question number you are attempting. Any rough work must be written in this booklet. Score through your rough work when you have written your final copy.

Use **blue** or **black** ink.

Before leaving the examination room you must give this booklet to the Invigilator; if you do not, you may lose all the marks for this paper.

SQA

SECTION 1 — 25 marks

The questions for Section 1 are contained in the question paper S857/75/02.

Read these and record your answers on the answer grid on *Page three* opposite.

Use **blue** or **black** ink. Do NOT use gel pens or pencil.

1. The answer to each question is **either** A, B, C, D or E. Decide what your answer is, then fill in the appropriate bubble (see sample question below).

2. There is **only one correct** answer to each question.

3. Any rough work must be written in the additional space for answers and rough work at the end of this booklet.

Sample Question

The energy unit measured by the electricity meter in your home is the

    A   ampere

    B   kilowatt-hour

    C   watt

    D   coulomb

    E   volt.

The correct answer is **B** — kilowatt-hour. The answer **B** bubble has been clearly filled in (see below).

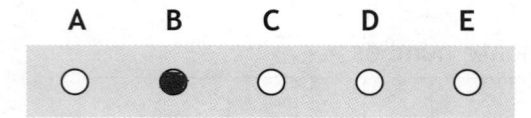

Changing an answer

If you decide to change your answer, cancel your first answer by putting a cross through it (see below) and fill in the answer you want. The answer below has been changed to **D**.

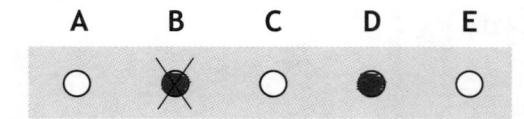

If you then decide to change back to an answer you have already scored out, put a tick (✓) to the **right** of the answer you want, as shown below:

SECTION 1 — Answer Grid

[BLANK PAGE]

DO NOT WRITE ON THIS PAGE

MARKS DO NOT WRITE IN THIS MARGIN

SECTION 2 — 110 marks

Attempt ALL questions

1. An aircraft is making a journey between two airports. A graph of the aircraft's velocity during take-off is shown.

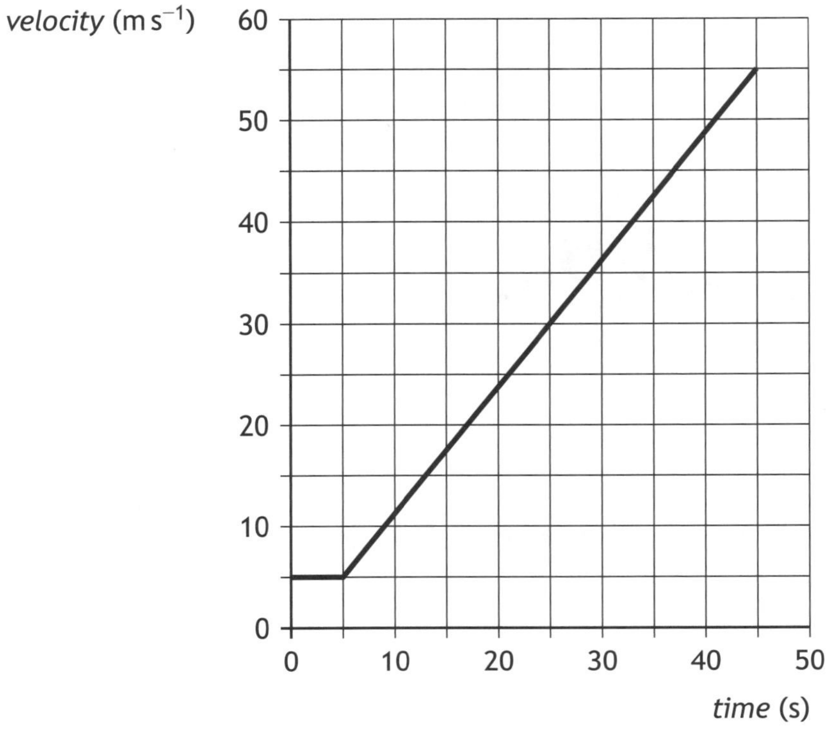

(a) Calculate the acceleration of the aircraft during take-off. **3**

Space for working and answer

1. (continued)

(b) During flight, the aircraft is travelling at a velocity of 150 m s⁻¹ due north and then encounters a crosswind of 40 m s⁻¹ due east.

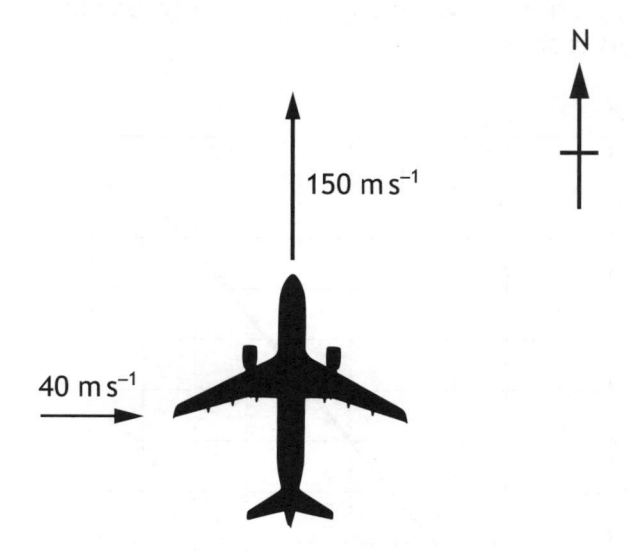

By scale diagram, or otherwise, determine:

(i) the magnitude of the resultant velocity of the aircraft; **2**

Space for working and answer

(ii) the direction of the resultant velocity of the aircraft. **2**

Space for working and answer

1. (continued)

   (c) The aircraft arrives at the destination airport.

   There are three runways, X, Y and Z, available for the aircraft to land on. The length of each runway is given in the table.

Runway	Length (m)
X	3776
Y	3048
Z	2743

   (i) The speed-time graph below shows the speed of the aircraft during landing on the runway, from the moment the wheels touch down.

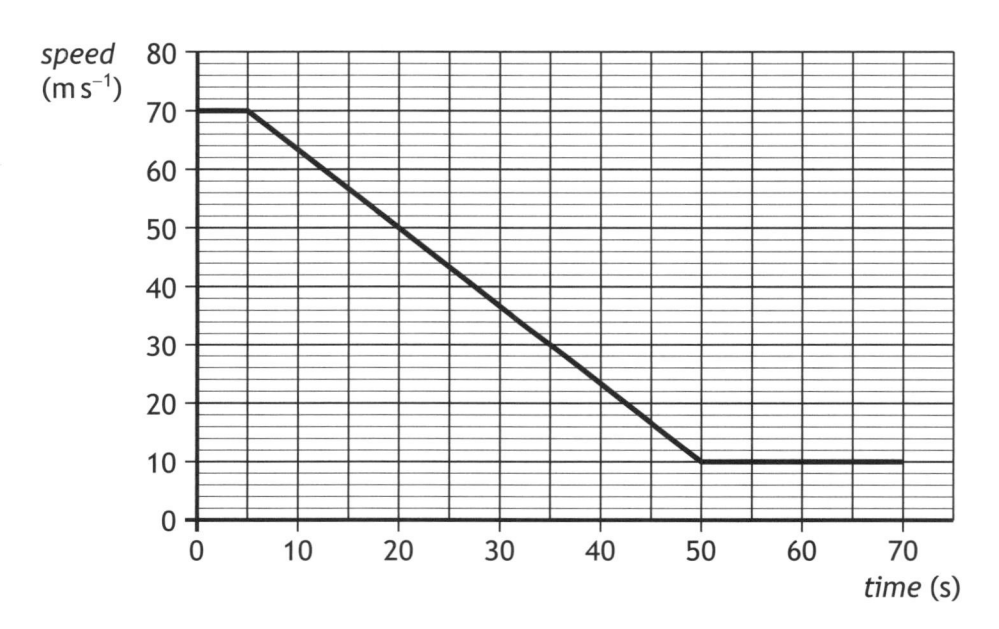

   Determine which runways the aircraft could have used to land safely.

   Justify your answer by calculation.

   Space for working and answer

1. (c) (continued)

(ii) This airport has runways of different lengths to accommodate different sizes of aircraft.

Explain why larger aircraft require a longer runway to land safely. **2**

2. The Soyuz Spacecraft is used to transport astronauts from the International Space Station (ISS) to Earth.

The spacecraft contains three parts.

Part	Mass (kg)
Orbital Module	1300
Descent Module (including astronauts)	2950
Instrumentation/Propulsion Module	2900

(a) When the spacecraft leaves the ISS, the three parts are launched together. The propulsion module produces a force of 1430 N.

Calculate the acceleration of the spacecraft as it leaves the ISS.

Space for working and answer

2. (continued)

(b) During the flight, the Orbital Module and the Instrumentation/Propulsion Module are jettisoned. Instead of returning to Earth, they burn up in the atmosphere at a very high temperature.

Explain why these Modules burn up on re-entry into the atmosphere. **2**

(c) (i) After the Descent Module has re-entered the atmosphere, its speed is dramatically reduced. Four parachutes are used to slow the Module's rate of descent.

Explain, in terms of forces, how the parachutes reduce the speed of the Module. **2**

2. (c) (continued)

(ii) Just before touchdown, small engines fire on the bottom of the Module, slowing it down further. The work done by the engines is 8.0×10^4 J over a distance of 5.0 m.

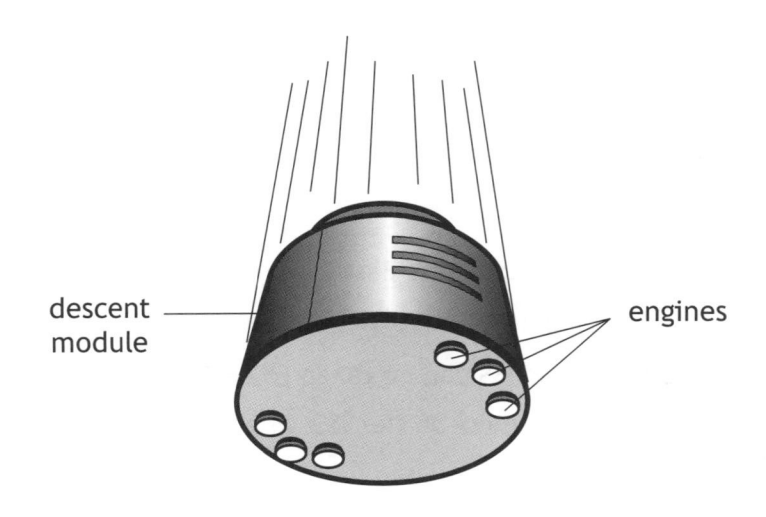

descent module — engines

Calculate the force produced by the engines.

Space for working and answer

2. (continued)

(d) The ISS orbits with an altitude of between 3.30×10^5 m and 4.35×10^5 m above the surface of the Earth.

(i) The orbital period T, in seconds, of the ISS can be calculated using the relationship

$$T = \frac{2\pi R}{v}$$

where v is the orbital speed in metres per second and R is the orbital radius in metres.

The orbital radius R is the sum of the radius of the Earth and the altitude above the surface of the Earth.

The radius of the Earth is 6.4×10^6 m.

The orbital speed of the ISS can be taken to be 7.7×10^3 m s^{-1}.

Calculate the orbital period of the ISS when it is orbiting at an altitude of 3.30×10^5 m.

Space for working and answer

(ii) State whether the orbital period of the ISS in its highest orbit will be less than, the same as, or greater than the orbital period calculated in part (d) (i).

(iii) Explain, in terms of its horizontal velocity and weight, how the ISS remains in orbit around the Earth.

3. Read the passage below about the Dragonfish nebula, an interstellar cloud of dust and gases and star-forming region in space. Answer the questions that follow.

> **Dragonfish nebula conceals giant cluster of young stars**
>
> The Dragonfish nebula may contain the Milky Way's most massive cluster of young stars. Scientists from the University of Toronto found the first hint of the cluster in 2010 in the form of a big cloud of ionised gas 30 000 light years from Earth. They detected the gas from its microwave emissions, suspecting that radiation from massive stars nearby had ionised the gas.
>
> Now the scientists have identified a cluster of 400 massive stars in the heart of the gas cloud using images from an infrared telescope. The cluster probably contains more stars which are too small and dim to detect.
>
> The surrounding cloud of ionised gas is producing more microwaves than the clouds around other star clusters in our galaxy. This suggests that the Dragonfish nebula contains the brightest and most massive young cluster discovered so far, with a total mass of around 100 000 times the mass of the Sun.

(a) Name the galaxy mentioned in the passage. 1

(b) Show that the Dragonfish nebula is approximately $2 \cdot 8 \times 10^{20}$ m away from Earth. 3

Space for working and answer

3. (continued)

(c) State how the frequency of microwave radiation compares to the frequency of infrared radiation. **1**

(d) A line spectrum from a nebula is shown below.

spectral lines from gases in the nebula

nitrogen

helium

hydrogen

krypton

Identify which of these elements are present in the nebula. **2**

4. In October 2012, a skydiver jumped from a balloon at a height of 39 km above the surface of the Earth.

He became the first person to jump from this height.

He also became the first human to fall at speeds higher than the speed of sound in air.

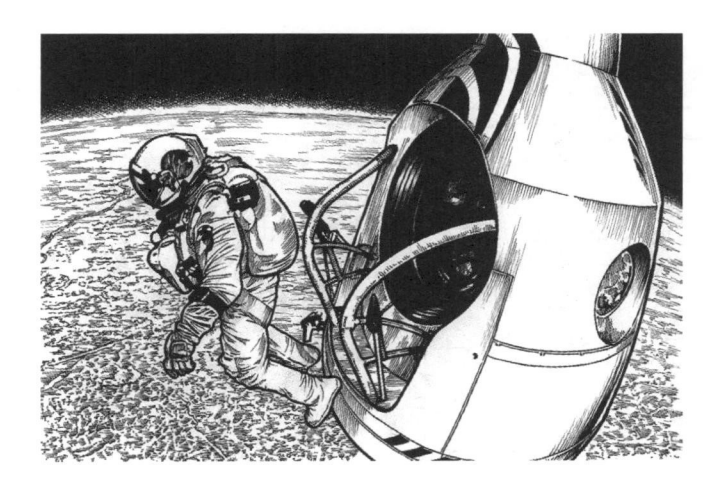

Using your knowledge of physics, comment on the challenges faced by the skydiver when making this jump.

3

5. (a) A student sets up the following circuit.

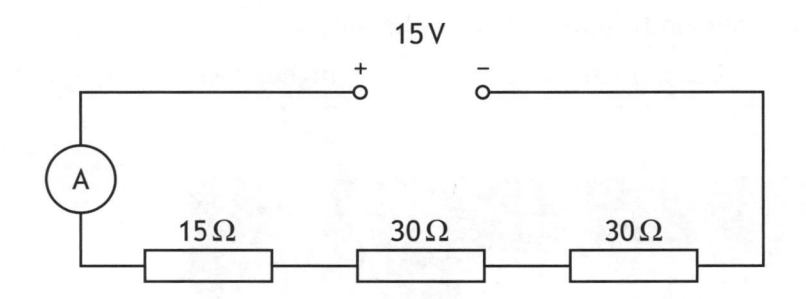

(i) Determine the total resistance in the circuit. [1]

(ii) Calculate the current in the circuit. [3]
Space for working and answer

(iii) Calculate the power dissipated in the 15 Ω resistor. [3]
Space for working and answer

5. (continued)

(b) The circuit is now rearranged as shown.

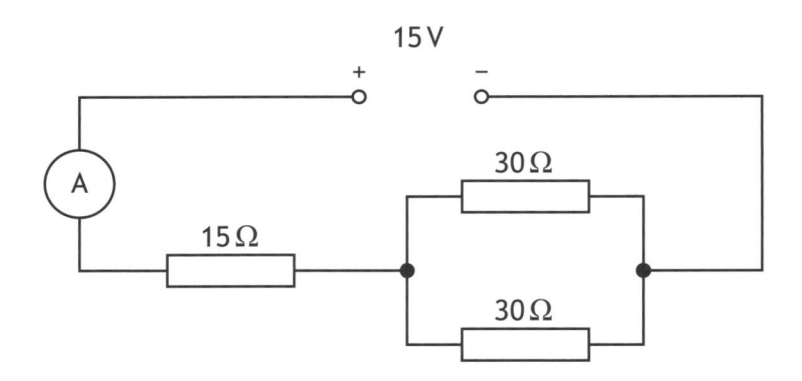

State how the power dissipated in the 15 Ω resistor compares to your answer in (a)(iii).

You must justify your answer. **3**

6. An office has an automatic window blind that closes when the light level outside gets too high.

The electronic circuit that operates the motor to close the blind is shown.

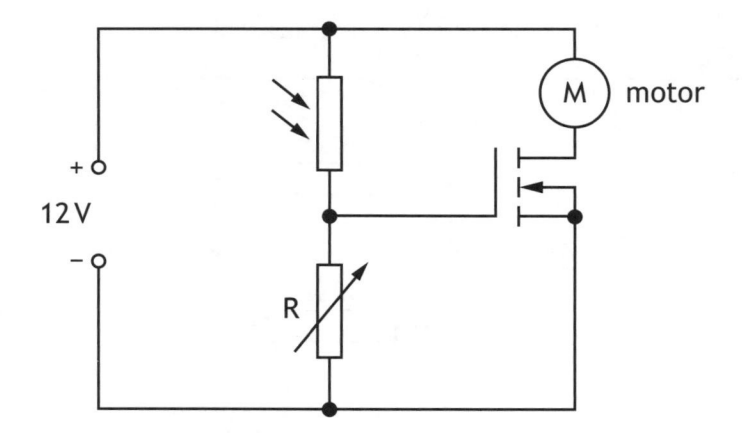

(a) The MOSFET switches on when the voltage across variable resistor R reaches 2·4 V.

   (i) Explain how this circuit works to close the blind. **3**

   (ii) What is the purpose of the variable resistor R? **1**

6. (continued)

(b) The graph shows how the resistance of the LDR varies with light level.

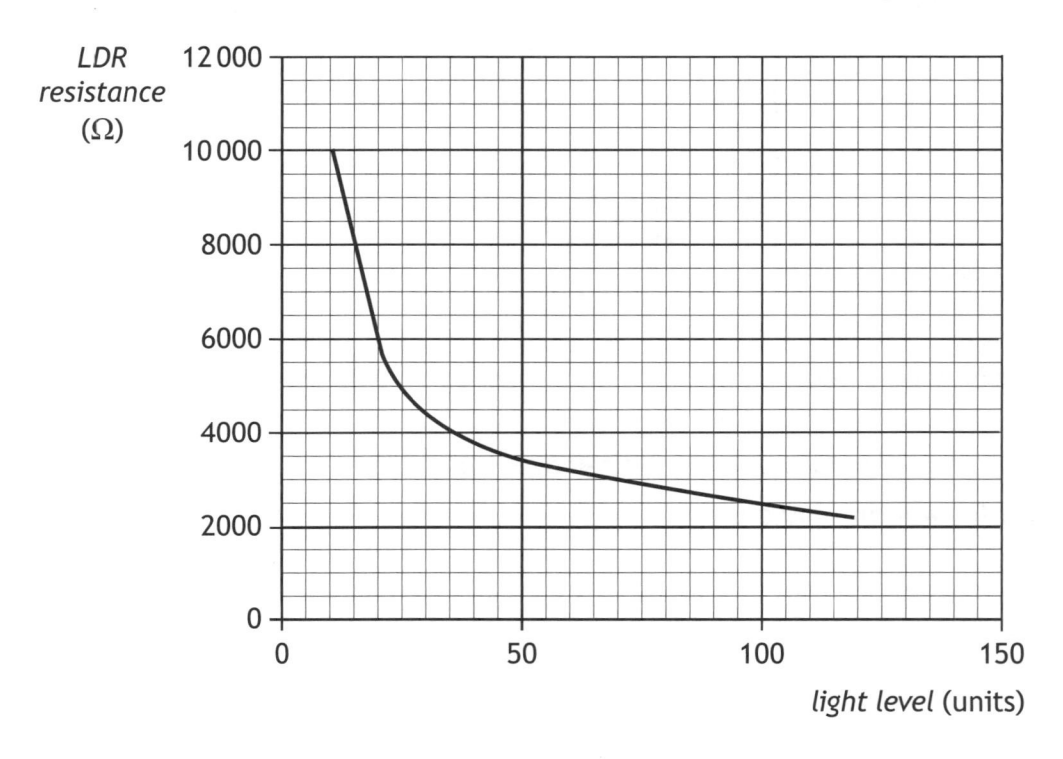

[Graph: LDR resistance (Ω) vs light level (units). Curve starts at ~10 000 Ω at low light, decreases steeply to ~3500 Ω around 50 units, then levels off to ~2200 Ω at 120 units.]

(i) Determine the resistance of the LDR when the light level is 70 units. **1**

(ii) The variable resistor R is set at a resistance of 600 Ω.
Calculate the voltage across R when the light level is 70 units. **3**
Space for working and answer

(iii) State whether or not the blinds will close when the light level is 70 units.
Justify your answer. **2**

7. A fridge/freezer has water and ice dispensers as shown.

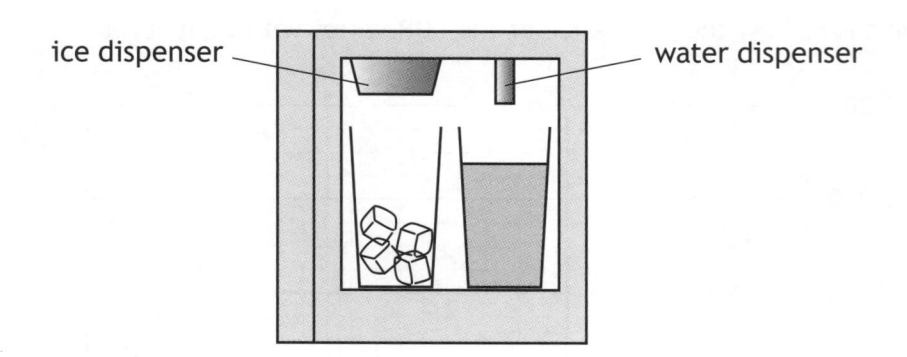

   (a) Water of mass 0·100 kg flows into the freezer at 15·0 °C and is cooled to 0 °C.

   Show that $6·27 \times 10^3$ J of energy is removed when the water cools.   **2**

   Space for working and answer

   (b) Calculate the energy released when 0·100 kg of water at 0 °C changes to 0·100 kg of ice at 0 °C.   **3**

   Space for working and answer

7. (continued)

(c) The fridge/freezer system removes heat energy at a rate of $115\,J\,s^{-1}$.

  (i) Calculate the minimum time taken to produce 0·100 kg of ice from 0·100 kg of water at 15·0 °C.

  Space for working and answer

  (ii) Explain why the actual time taken to make the ice will be longer than the time calculated in part (c)(i).

8. A student carries out an experiment to investigate the relationship between the pressure and volume of a fixed mass of gas using the apparatus shown.

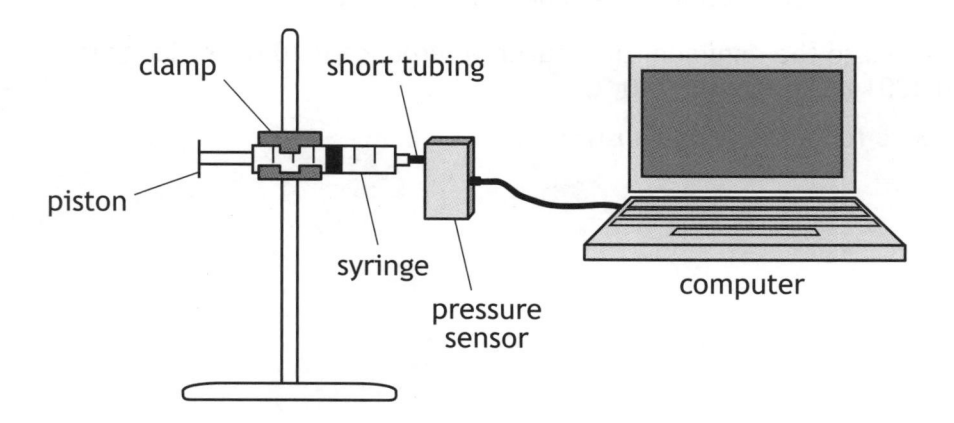

The pressure p of the gas is recorded using a pressure sensor connected to a computer. The volume V of the gas in the syringe is also recorded. The student pushes the piston to alter the volume and a series of readings is taken.

The temperature of the gas is constant during the experiment.

The results are shown.

p (kPa)	100	125	152	185	200
V (cm³)	50	40	33	27	25
$1/V$ (cm⁻³)	0·020	0·025	0·030	0·037	0·040

(a) (i) Using the square-ruled paper on *Page twenty-three*, draw a graph of p against $1/V$.

You must start the scale on each axis from 0.   **3**

(Additional square-ruled paper, if required, can be found on *Page thirty-two*.)

(ii) Explain how the graph confirms that pressure is directly proportional to 1/volume.   **1**

8. (a) (continued)

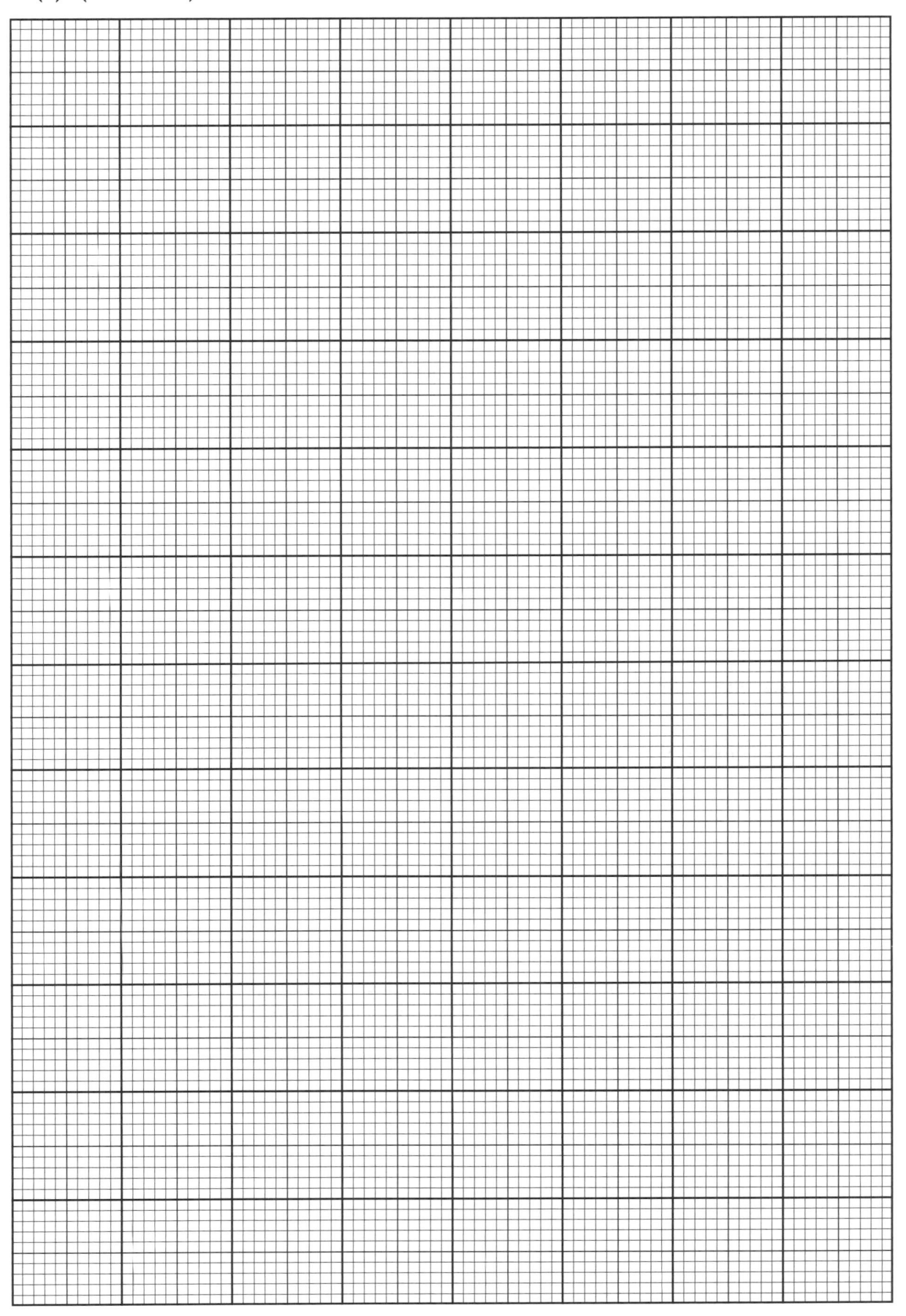

8. (continued)

(b) Calculate the pressure of the gas in the syringe when its volume is 8·0 cm³.

Space for working and answer

(c) Using the kinetic model, explain the increase in the pressure of the gas in the syringe as its volume decreases.

(d) (i) When carrying out the experiment, the student clamped the syringe rather than holding it in their hand.

Explain why this is better experimental practice.

(ii) A second student suggests that replacing the short tubing between the syringe and the pressure sensor with one of longer length would improve the experiment.

Explain why this student's suggestion is incorrect.

9. A mountain climber carries a small, portable device which receives radio signals from satellites to determine the climber's position.

   The device can also be used to send the climber's position to the emergency services in the event of an accident.

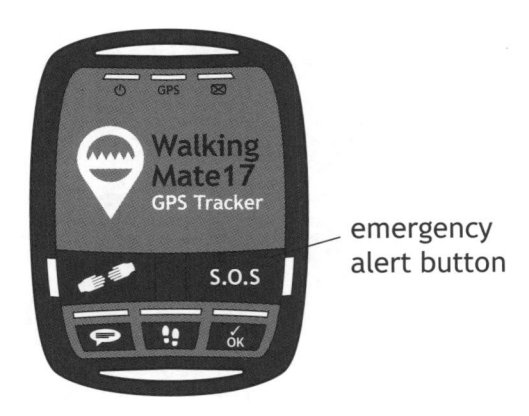

   (a) One satellite sends a radio signal that is received by the device 0·0047 s after transmission.

   (i) State the speed of the radio signal. **1**

   (ii) Calculate the distance between this satellite and the climber. **3**

   Space for working and answer

   (b) The device sends a radio signal via satellite to the emergency services.

   The frequency of the signal is 1620 MHz.

   Calculate the wavelength of this signal. **3**

   Space for working and answer

9. (continued)

(c)

mobile phone transmitter

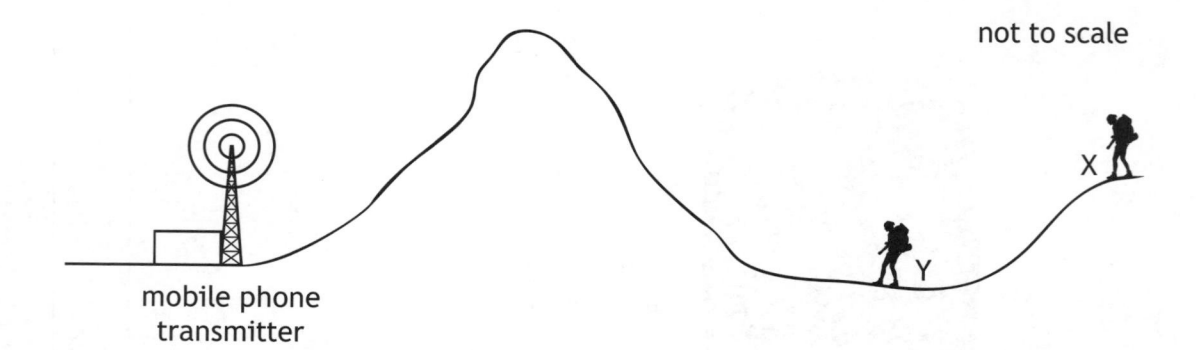

not to scale

The climber also carries a mobile phone. The climber notices that the phone receives a signal at X but not at Y.

Explain why the phone receives a signal at X but not at Y. 2

10. A physics textbook contains the following statement.

'Electromagnetic waves can be sent out like ripples on a pond.'

Using your knowledge of physics, comment on the similarities and/or differences between electromagnetic waves and the ripples on a pond.

3

11. Trees continually absorb carbon-14 when they are alive. When a tree dies the carbon-14 contained in its wood is not replaced. Carbon-14 is radioactive and decays by beta emission.

(a) Following the tree's death, the activity of the carbon-14 within a **25 mg** sample of its wood changes as shown.

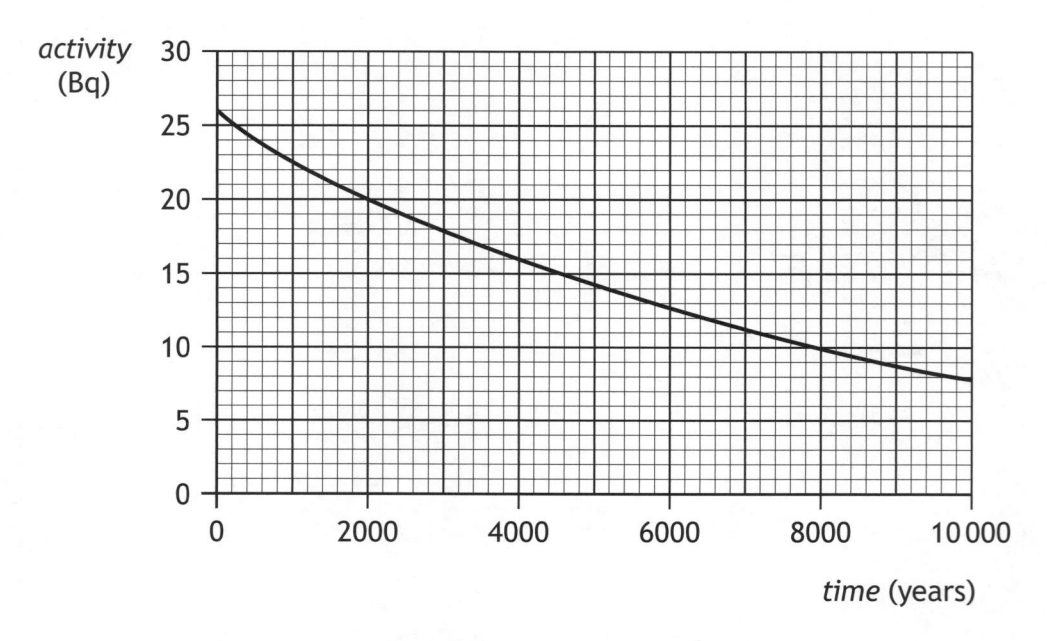

(i) Use the graph to determine the half-life of carbon-14. **1**

(ii) Calculate the time taken for the activity of this sample of carbon-14 to fall to 6·5 Bq. **3**

Space for working and answer

11. (a) (continued)

(iii) During an archaeological dig, a 125 mg sample of the same type of wood was obtained. The activity of this sample was 40 Bq.

Estimate the age of this sample. **3**

Space for working and answer

(b) Explain why this method could not be used to estimate the age of a tree that died 100 years ago. **1**

12. A worker in the radiation industry uses a radioactive source to investigate the effect of gamma rays on biological tissue.

(a) State what is meant by the term *gamma rays*. **[1]**

(b) In one experiment, a biological tissue sample of mass 0·10 kg receives an absorbed dose of 50 µGy.

Calculate the energy absorbed by the tissue. **[3]**

Space for working and answer

(c) The radioactive source must be stored in a lead-lined container.

Explain why a lead-lined container should be used. **[1]**

12. (continued)

(d) State the annual effective dose limit for the radiation worker.

1

[END OF SPECIMEN QUESTION PAPER]

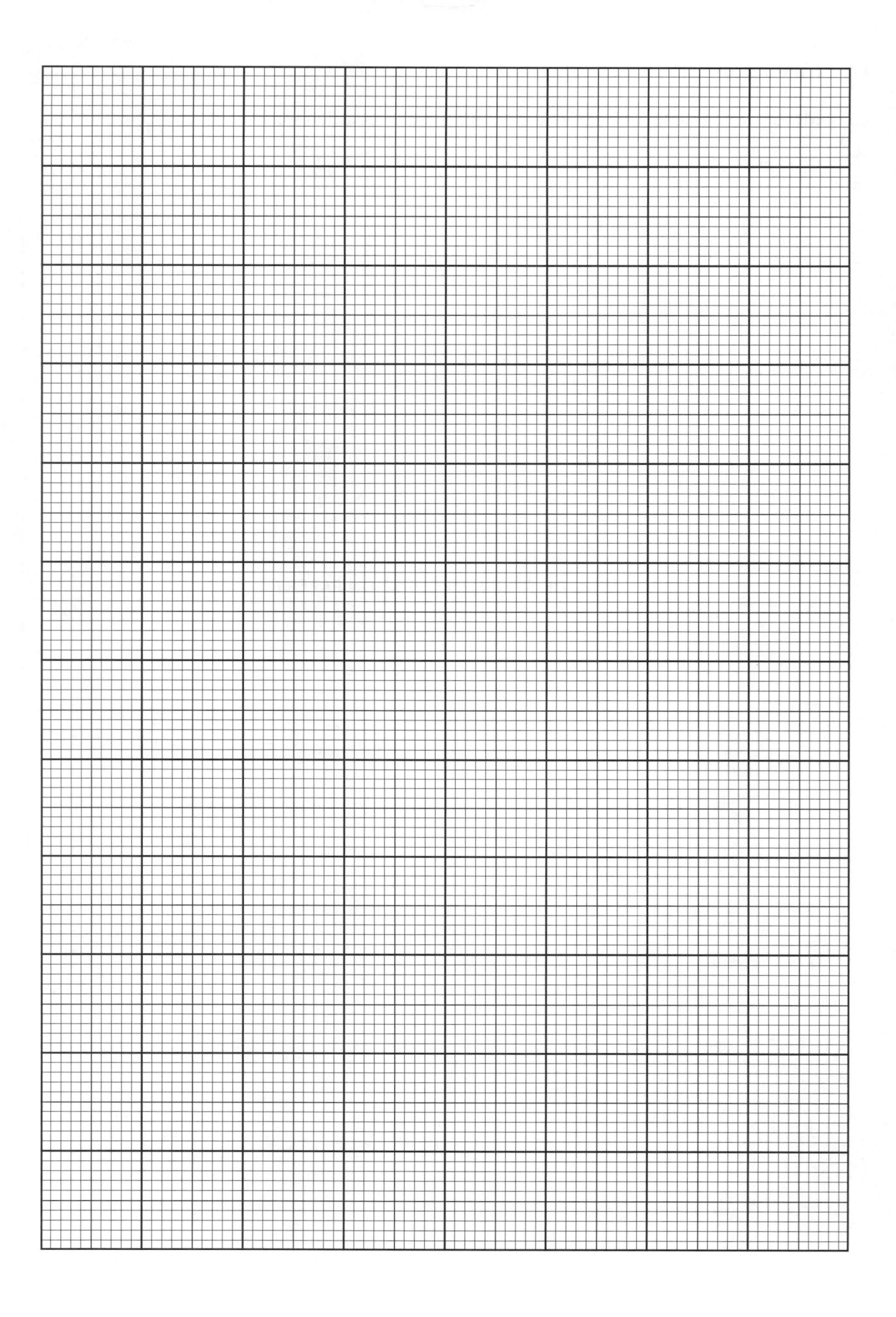

ADDITIONAL SPACE FOR ANSWERS AND ROUGH WORKING

ADDITIONAL SPACE FOR ANSWERS AND ROUGH WORKING

NATIONAL 5
Answers

SQA NATIONAL 5 PHYSICS 2017

NATIONAL 5 PHYSICS 2015

Section 1

1.	A	6.	D	11.	E	16.	C
2.	A	7.	D	12.	A	17.	A
3.	C	8.	A	13.	E	18.	B
4.	E	9.	C	14.	C	19.	E
5.	B	10.	E	15.	B	20.	D

Section 2

1. (a) 2 marks for symbols:
   - All correct — 2
   - At least two different symbols correct — 1

   1 mark for correct representation of external circuit wiring with no gaps

   (b) $V = IR$ — 1
   $2 \cdot 5 = 0 \cdot 5 \times R$ — 1
   $R = 5\,\Omega$

   (c) Mark for effect can only be awarded if a justification is attempted.

   Incorrect or no effect stated, regardless of justification — no marks.

   Effect:
   (It/lamp L is) brighter — 1

   Justification:
   M is in parallel (with resistor) — 1
   Greater current in/through lamp L (than that in M) — 1

   OR

   Effect:
   (It/lamp L is) brighter — 1

   Justification:
   M is in parallel (with resistor) — 1
   Greater voltage across lamp L (than across M) — 1

2. (a) (Graph) X — 1
   An LED/diode/it only conducts in one direction — 1

   (b) (i) $P = IV$ — 1
   $P = 0 \cdot 5 \times 4$
   $P = 2\,(W)$

   $E = Pt$ — 1
   $E = 2 \times 60$ — 1
   $E = 120\,J$ — 1

   (ii) $Q = I \times t$ — 1
   $Q = 0 \cdot 5 \times 60$ — 1
   $Q = 30\,C$ — 1

3. (a) (i) 15 μs
   (ii) **Method 1:**
   $d = vt$ — 1
   $= 5200 \times 15 \times 10^{-6}$ — 1
   $= 0 \cdot 078\,(m)$ — 1

   (If this line is the final answer then unit required for mark)
   $thickness = \dfrac{0 \cdot 078}{2}$
   $= 0 \cdot 039\,m$ — 1

   Method 2:
   $time = \dfrac{15 \times 10^{-6}}{2}$
   $= 7 \cdot 5 \times 10^{-6}\,(s)$ — 1
   $d = vt$ — 1
   $= 5200 \times 7 \cdot 5 \times 10^{-6}$ — 1
   $= 0 \cdot 039\,m$ — 1

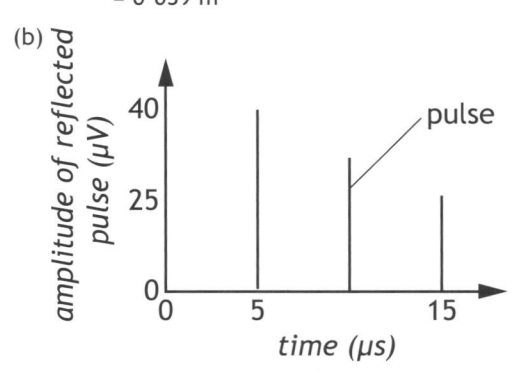

   (b)

   [Graph: amplitude of reflected pulse (μV) vs time (μs). Pulses shown at approximately 0, 5 μs (amplitude 40), and a labelled "pulse" between 5 and 15 μs at amplitude ~25-30]

   1 mark is awarded for "a peak at a time greater than 5 μs and less than 15 μs"
   and
   1 mark is awarded for "an amplitude greater than 25 μV and less than 40 μV"

   (c) (i) This is a "show that" question so must start with correct formula or zero marks.
   $f = \dfrac{1}{T}$ — 1
   $= \dfrac{1}{4 \cdot 0 \times 10^{-6}}$ — 1
   $= 2 \cdot 5 \times 10^5\,Hz$

   (ii) $v = f\lambda$ — 1
   $5200 = 2 \cdot 5 \times 10^5 \times \lambda$ — 1
   $\lambda = 0 \cdot 021\,m$ — 1

   (d) Mark for effect can only be awarded if a justification is attempted.

   Incorrect or no effect stated, regardless of justification — no marks.

   (Speed of ultrasound in brass is) less (than in steel). — 1
   Takes greater time to travel (same) distance/thickness. — 1

4. Demonstrates no understanding — 0 marks
Demonstrates limited understanding — 1 mark
Demonstrates reasonable understanding — 2 marks
Demonstrates good understanding — 3 marks

This is an open-ended question.

1 mark: The student has demonstrated a limited understanding of the physics involved. The student has made some statement(s) which is/are relevant to the situation, showing that at least a little of the physics within the problem is understood.

2 marks: The student has demonstrated a reasonable understanding of the physics involved. The student makes some statement(s) which is/are relevant to the situation, showing that the problem is understood.

3 marks: The maximum available mark would be awarded to a student who has demonstrated a good understanding of the physics involved. The student shows a good comprehension of the physics of the situation and has provided a logically correct answer to the question posed. This type of response might include a statement of the principles involved, a relationship or an equation, and the application of these to respond to the problem. This does not mean the answer has to be what might be termed an "excellent" answer or a "complete" one.

5. (a) Correctly labelled the angle of incidence **and** angle of refraction

   (b) Decreases

   (c) B

   (d) $P = \dfrac{F}{A}$ — 1

   $= \dfrac{61000}{1 \cdot 1 \times 10^{-5}}$ — 1

   $= 5 \cdot 5 \times 10^{9}$ Pa — 1

6. (a) Increases

   (b) (i) Mark for choice can only be awarded if an explanation is attempted.

   Incorrect or no choice made, regardless of explanation — no marks.

   Choice:

   (source) X — 1

   Explanation:

   beta (source required) — 1

   long half-life — 1

   (ii) Time for activity to (decrease by) half

   OR

   Time for half the nuclei to decay

   (iii) (high frequency) electromagnetic wave

   (c) 2 hours

7. (a) (i) **Using Pythagoras:**

   $\text{Resultant}^2 = (6 \cdot 0 \times 10^3)^2 + (8 \cdot 0 \times 10^3)^2$ — 1

   $\text{Resultant} = 10 \times 10^3$ N — 1

   Using scale diagram:

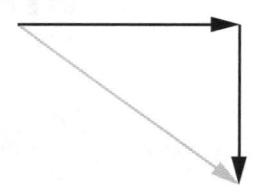

   vectors to scale — 1

   Resultant $= 10 \times 10^3$ N — 1

   (allow $\pm 0 \cdot 5 \times 10^3$ N tolerance)

   (ii) **Using trigonometry:**

   $\tan \theta = 6/8$ — 1

   $\theta = 37°$ — 1

   Using scale diagram:

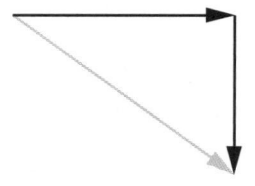

   angles correct — 1

   $\theta = 37°$ — 1

   (allow $\pm 2°$ tolerance)

   (iii) $F = ma$ — 1

   $10 \times 10^3 = 5 \cdot 0 \times 10^6 \times a$ — 1

   $a = 2 \cdot 0 \times 10^{-3}$ m s^{-2} — 1

   (b) **Upward arrow:** buoyancy force/upthrust/force of water on ship/flotation force — 1

   Downward arrow: weight/force of gravity — 1

   (These) forces are balanced — 1

8. (a) (i) • length/width of card — 1
   • time taken for card to pass (through) the light gate — 1
   • time taken (for trolley to travel from starting position) to light gate — 1

   (ii) reaction time (can cause error with the stop clock reading)

   OR

   card may not have passed straight through light gate

   OR

   length/width of card not measured properly (e.g. ruler not straight along card)

   OR

   other suitable reason

(b) $a = \dfrac{v-u}{t}$ 1

$= \dfrac{1 \cdot 6 - 0}{2 \cdot 5}$ 1

$= 0 \cdot 64 \text{ m s}^{-2}$ 1

9. (a) suitable curved path   1

(b) (i) $a = \dfrac{v-u}{t}$ 1

$9 \cdot 8 = \dfrac{v - 0}{0 \cdot 80}$ 1

$v = 7 \cdot 8 \text{ m s}^{-1}$ 1

(ii) $\bar{v} = 3 \cdot 9 \text{ m s}^{-1}$ 1

$d = \bar{v} t$ 1

$= 3 \cdot 9 \times 0 \cdot 80$ 1

$= 3 \cdot 1 \text{ m}$ 1

(c) (it will take the) same (time)

10. Demonstrates no understanding   0 marks

Demonstrates limited understanding   1 mark

Demonstrates reasonable understanding   2 marks

Demonstrates good understanding   3 marks

This is an open-ended question.

1 mark: The student has demonstrated a limited understanding of the physics involved. The student has made some statement(s) which is/are relevant to the situation, showing that at least a little of the physics within the problem is understood.

2 marks: The student has demonstrated a reasonable understanding of the physics involved. The student makes some statement(s) which is/are relevant to the situation, showing that the problem is understood.

3 marks: The maximum available mark would be awarded to a student who has demonstrated a good understanding of the physics involved. The student shows a good comprehension of the physics of the situation and has provided a logically correct answer to the question posed. This type of response might include a statement of the principles involved, a relationship or an equation, and the application of these to respond to the problem. This does not mean the answer has to be what might be termed an "excellent" answer or a "complete" one.

11. (a) (i) $E_p = mgh$ 1

$E_p = 0 \cdot 040 \times 9 \cdot 8 \times 0 \cdot 50$ 1

$E_p = 0 \cdot 20 \text{ J}$ 1

(ii) kinetic (energy) to heat (and sound)

OR

kinetic (energy) of the marble to kinetic (energy) of the sand.

(b) (i) suitable scales, labels and units   1

all points plotted accurately to ± half a division   1

best fit <u>curve</u>   1

(ii) Consistent with best fit curve from (b)(i).

(iii) Any two from:

- Repeat (and average)
- Take (more) readings in the 0·15 (m) to 0·35 (m) drop height range
- Increase the height range
- level sand between drops
- or other suitable improvement

(1) each

(c) (i) suitable variable

e.g.

- mass/weight of marble
- angle of impact
- type of sand
- diameter of marble
- radius of marble
- density of marble
- volume of marble
- speed of marble
- time of drop

(ii) How independent variable can be measured/changed   1

State at least one other variable to be controlled   1

NATIONAL 5 PHYSICS 2017

Section 1
1.	A	6.	D	11.	B	16.	E
2.	D	7.	B	12.	A	17.	D
3.	A	8.	E	13.	B	18.	B
4.	E	9.	C	14.	C	19.	B
5.	B	10.	C	15.	C	20.	D

Section 2

1. (a) (i) [resistor symbol] — 1

   (ii) stops too large a current — 1
   OR prevents wiring overheating
   OR protect wiring (from damage)

   (iii) 3 A (fuse required) — 1
   $P = IV$ — 1
   $290 = I \times 230$ — 1
   $I = 1\cdot 3 (A)$ — 1

   (b) direction of electron (flow) (continually) changing back and forth/to and fro — 1

2. (a) (i) $R_T = 40\cdot 0\ (\Omega)$ — 1
   $V = IR$ — 1
   $12\cdot 0 = I \times 40\cdot 0$
   $(I = 0\cdot 300\ A)$
   $V = IR$
   $= 0\cdot 300 \times 25\cdot 0$ for all substitutions — 1
   $= 7\cdot 50\ V$ — 1

   (ii) $P = \dfrac{V^2}{R}$ — 1
   $= \dfrac{7\cdot 50^2}{25\cdot 0}$ — 1
   $= 2\cdot 25\ W$ — 1

   (b) (i) $\dfrac{1}{R_T} = \dfrac{1}{R_1} + \dfrac{1}{R_2}$ — 1
   $= \dfrac{1}{15\cdot 0} + \dfrac{1}{35\cdot 0}$ — 1
   $R_T = 10\cdot 5\ \Omega$ — 1

   (ii) (power dissipated is) greater/increased/higher — 1
   (combined/parallel/total) resistance less — 1
   voltage across motor is greater/increased
   OR
   current (in motor) is greater/increased — 1

3. (a) $p_1 V_1 = p_2 V_2$ — 1
   $1\cdot 0 \times 10^5 \times 4\cdot 0 \times 10^{-4} = p_2 \times 1\cdot 6 \times 10^{-4}$ — 1
   $p_2 = 2\cdot 5 \times 10^5\ Pa$ — 1

   (b) (individual) particles collide with container/walls more frequently (than before) — 1
   (overall) force (on walls) is greater — 1
   pressure increases — 1

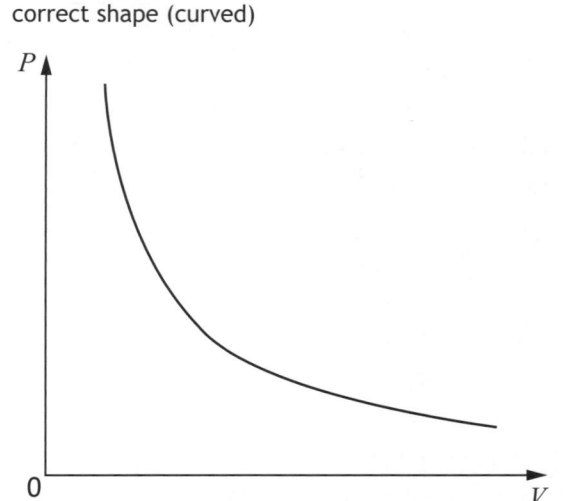

   (c) axes labelled p and V — 1
   correct shape (curved) — 1

   [graph of P vs V, curve decreasing]

4. (a) (i) $T = \dfrac{1}{f}$ — 1
   $2\cdot 5 = \dfrac{1}{f}$ — 1
   $f = 0\cdot 40\ Hz$ — 1

   (ii) measure the time for more waves to pass
   OR
   count the number of waves in a longer period of time — 1
   OR
   repeat (the measurement) and average

   (b) $v = f\lambda$ — 1
   $v = 0\cdot 40 \times 8\cdot 0$ — 1
   $v = 3\cdot 2\ m\,s^{-1}$ — 1

   (c) diffraction of waves into 'shadow' regions behind walls — 1
   straight sections in middle and consistent wavelengths before and after gap — 1

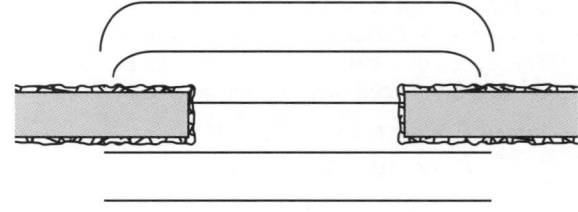

   [diagram of waves diffracting through gap]

   (d) <u>energy</u> decreases/lost — 1

5. Demonstrates no understanding — 0 marks
   Demonstrates limited understanding — 1 mark
   Demonstrates reasonable understanding — 2 marks
   Demonstrates good understanding — 3 marks

   This is an open-ended question.

   1 mark: The student has demonstrated a limited understanding of the physics involved. The student has made some statement(s) which is/are relevant to the situation, showing that at least a little of the physics within the problem is understood.

… ANSWERS FOR NATIONAL 5 PHYSICS   167

2 marks: The student has demonstrated a reasonable understanding of the physics involved. The student makes some statement(s) which is/are relevant to the situation, showing that the problem is understood.

3 marks: The maximum available mark would be awarded to a student who has demonstrated a good understanding of the physics involved. The student shows a good comprehension of the physics of the situation and has provided a logically correct answer to the question posed. This type of response might include a statement of the principles involved, a relationship or an equation, and the application of these to respond to the problem. This does not mean the answer has to be what might be termed an "excellent" answer or a "complete" one.

6. (a) background count (rate)   1

   (b) (i) 4·4 mm

   (ii) Evidence of establishing 3 half-value thicknesses   1

   (3 × 4·4)

   13·2 mm   1

   (iii) greater   1

   (c) $\dot{H} = \dfrac{H}{t}$ 1

   $2\cdot5 \times 10^{-6} = \dfrac{20 \times 10^{-3}}{t}$ 1

   $t = 8000$ (h)   1

7. (a) 80 000 (nuclei) decay(s) per unit time   1

   (b) (i) neutrons can go on to cause further (fission) reactions/split more (uranium) nuclei   1

   causing a chain reaction/this process repeats   1

   (ii) $(E) = 3\cdot0 \times 10^{21} \times 3\cdot2 \times 10^{-11}$ 1

   $= (9\cdot6 \times 10^{10}$ J)

   $P = \dfrac{E}{t}$ 1

   $= \dfrac{9\cdot6 \times 10^{10}}{60}$ 1

   $= 1\cdot6 \times 10^{9}$ W   1

   (c) any suitable use   1

   (eg treating cancer/tracers/sterilisation/smoke detectors/measuring thickness of paper)

8. (a) 0 (m)   1

   (b) (i) d = area under graph   1

   $= (0\cdot5 \times 1 \times 3) + (0\cdot5 \times 3 \times 24) + (3 \times 3)$ 1

   $= 46\cdot5$ m   1

   (ii) $a = \dfrac{v - u}{t}$ 1

   $a = \dfrac{27 - 3}{3\cdot0}$ 1

   $a = 8$ m s^{-2} 1

   (c) $d = \bar{v}t$ 1

   $4 \times 380 = \bar{v} \times 79$ 1

   $\bar{v} = 19$ m s^{-1} 1

9. (a) (The forces are) equal (in size) and opposite (in direction).   1

   (b) $W = mg$ 1

   $1176 = m \times 9\cdot8$ 1

   $m = 120$ kg   1

   (c) $F = 1344 - 1176 = 168$ (N)   1

   $F = ma$ 1

   $168 = 120 \times a$ 1

   $a = 1\cdot4$ m s^{-2} 1

10. Demonstrates no understanding   0 marks

    Demonstrates limited understanding   1 mark

    Demonstrates reasonable understanding   2 marks

    Demonstrates good understanding   3 marks

    This is an open-ended question.

    1 mark: The student has demonstrated a limited understanding of the physics involved. The student has made some statement(s) which is/are relevant to the situation, showing that at least a little of the physics within the problem is understood.

    2 marks: The student has demonstrated a reasonable understanding of the physics involved. The student makes some statement(s) which is/are relevant to the situation, showing that the problem is understood.

    3 marks: The maximum available mark would be awarded to a student who has demonstrated a good understanding of the physics involved. The student shows a good comprehension of the physics of the situation and has provided a logically correct answer to the question posed. This type of response might include a statement of the principles involved, a relationship or an equation, and the application of these to respond to the problem. This does not mean the answer has to be what might be termed an "excellent" answer or a "complete" one.

11. (a) Q   1

    (b) equal (to)   1

    vertical/downward acceleration is the same   1

    (c) $E_w = Fd$ 1

    $5500 = F \times 25$ 1

    $F = 220$ N   1

12. (a) (i) $3\cdot0 \times 10^{8}$ m s^{-1} 1

    (ii) $d = vt$ 1

    $d = 3\cdot0 \times 10^{8}$

    $\times (7\cdot8 \times 365\cdot25 \times 24 \times 60 \times 60)$ 1

    $d = 7\cdot4 \times 10^{16}$ (m)   1

    (b) (i) photographic film   1

    (ii) equal (to)   1

NATIONAL 5 PHYSICS
2017 SPECIMEN QUESTION PAPER

Section 1

1. D	6. C	11. C	16. C	21. E
2. A	7. D	12. D	17. A	22. A
3. B	8. D	13. B	18. B	23. E
4. A	9. B	14. C	19. A	24. B
5. C	10. A	15. B	20. A	25. E

Section 2

1. (a) $a = \dfrac{v-u}{t}$ 1

    $a = \dfrac{55-5}{40}$ 1

    $a = 1 \cdot 25 \text{ m s}^{-2}$ 1

   (b) (i) Scale diagram 2

    $v = 155 \pm 3 \text{ m s}^{-1}$

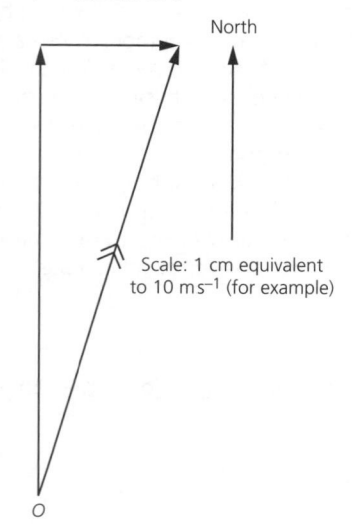

    OR

    Using Pythagoras:

    $v = \sqrt{150^2 + 40^2}$ 1

    $v = 155 \text{ m s}^{-1}$ 1

    Accept 150, 155·2, 155·24

   (ii) Scale diagram 2

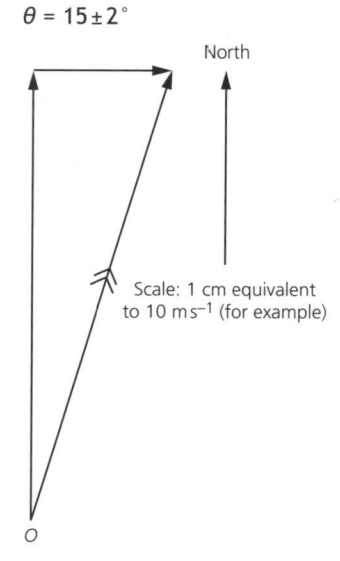

    $\theta = 15 \pm 2°$

    OR

    Using trigonometry:

    $\tan \theta = \dfrac{40}{150}$ 1

    $\theta = 15°$ 1

    Accept 10, 14·9, 14·93

    Bearing 015

    15° E of N

   (c) (i) s = area under $v - t$ graph 1

    $s = (10 \times 70) + (60 \times 5) + \dfrac{1}{2}(60 \times 45)$ 1

    $s = 2350$ (m) 1

    Runways X, Y and Z could have been used 1

   (ii) Aircraft has increased mass 1

    so has reduced deceleration 1

    OR

    Aircraft has increased kinetic energy 1

    $E_w = Fd$ (so if F is constant d is greater) 1

2. (a) $m = 1300 + 2950 + 2900$ 1

    $F = ma$ 1

    $1430 = (1300 + 2950 + 2900) \times a$ 1

    $a = 0 \cdot 2 \text{ m s}^{-2}$ 1

   (b) Force of friction is created on the surface of the modules 1

    causes heat to be produced 1

   (c) (i) Upward force is increased (by parachutes) 1

    producing an unbalanced force upwards 1

   (ii) $E_w = Fd$ 1

    $80\,000 = F \times 5$ 1

    $F = 16\,000 \text{ N}$ 1

   (d) (i) $T = \dfrac{2\pi R}{v}$

    $T = \dfrac{2 \times \pi \times (6 \cdot 4 \times 10^6 + 3 \cdot 30 \times 10^5)}{7 \cdot 7 \times 10^3}$ 1,1

    $T = 5500 \text{ s}$ 1

   (ii) (Orbital period will be) greater 1

   (iii) The horizontal velocity of the ISS is large enough to ensure that it does not get closer to the Earth's surface (or equivalent statement) 1

    The weight of the ISS is large enough to ensure that it does not move further away from the Earth's surface (or equivalent statement) 1

3. (a) Milky Way 1

   (b) $d = vt$ 1

    $d = 30\,000 \times 3 \times 10^8 \times (365 \cdot 25 \times 24 \times 60 \times 60)$ 1,1

    $d = 2 \cdot 8 \times 10^{20} \text{ m}$

   (c) (Microwave radiation has a) smaller (frequency than infra-red radiation) 1

   (d) Hydrogen 1

    Helium 1

… ANSWERS FOR NATIONAL 5 PHYSICS   169

4. Demonstrates no understanding — 0 marks
    Demonstrates limited understanding — 1 mark
    Demonstrates reasonable understanding — 2 marks
    Demonstrates good understanding — 3 marks

    This is an open-ended question.

    1 mark: The candidate has demonstrated a limited understanding of the physics involved. The candidate has made some statement(s) which is/are relevant to the situation, showing that at least a little of the physics within the problem is understood.

    2 marks: The candidate has demonstrated a reasonable understanding of the physics involved. The candidate makes some statement(s) which is/are relevant to the situation, showing that the problem is understood.

    3 marks: Award the maximum available mark to a candidate who has demonstrated a good understanding of the physics involved. The candidate shows a good comprehension of the physics of the situation and has provided a logically correct answer to the question posed. This type of response might include a statement of the principles involved, a relationship or an equation, and the application of these to respond to the problem. This does not mean the answer has to be what might be termed an 'excellent' answer or a 'complete' one.

5. (a) (i) $R_T = 75\,\Omega$ — 1
    (ii) $V = IR$ — 1
    $15 = I \times 75$ — 1
    $I = 0{\cdot}20\,\text{A}$ — 1
    (iii) $P = I^2R$ — 1
    $P = 0{\cdot}20^2 \times 15$ — 1
    $P = 0{\cdot}60\,\text{W}$ — 1
    (b) (The power dissipated is) greater (than that in (a)(iii)) — 1
    The total resistance of the circuit is now less — 1
    The current in the circuit is now greater — 1

6. (a) (i) Light level increases, LDR resistance decreases — 1
    LDR resistance decreases, voltage across R increases — 1
    Voltage across R increases, MOSFET switches the motor on — 1
    (ii) The variable resistor controls the light level at which the motor operates the blind — 1
    (b) (i) $3000 \pm 250\,\Omega$ — 1
    (ii) $V_2 = \left(\dfrac{R_2}{R_1 + R_2}\right)V_s$ — 1
    $V_2 = \left(\dfrac{600}{600 + 3000}\right) \times 12$ — 1
    $V_2 = 2{\cdot}0\,\text{V}$ — 1
    (iii) The blinds will not close — 1
    The voltage across R is insufficient to switch the MOSFET on — 1

7. (a) $E_h = cm\Delta T$ — 1
    $E_h = 4180 \times 0{\cdot}100 \times (15{\cdot}0 - 0)$ — 1
    $E_h = 6270\,\text{J}$
    (b) $E_h = ml$ — 1
    $E_h = 0{\cdot}100 \times 3{\cdot}34 \times 10^5$ — 1
    $E_h = 3{\cdot}34 \times 10^4\,\text{J}$ — 1

    (c) (i) $E_h = 6270 + 3{\cdot}34 \times 10^4\,(\text{J})$ — 1
    $P = \dfrac{E_h}{t}$ — 1
    $115 = \dfrac{(6270 + 3{\cdot}34 \times 10^4)}{t}$ — 1
    $t = 345\,\text{s}$ — 1
    (ii) Heat will be taken in from the surroundings — 1
    so the system will have additional heat to remove — 1

8. (a) (i) Axes labelled with units — 1
    Axes scaled linearly — 1
    Data points accurately plotted with line of best fit — 1
    (ii) The line of best fit is a straight line which passes through the origin — 1
    (b) $p_1V_1 = p_2V_2$ — 1
    $125 \times 40 = p_2 \times 8{\cdot}0$ — 1
    $p_2 = 630\,\text{kPa}$ — 1
    (c) As volume decreases, the particles of gas will strike the piston of the syringe more often — 1
    Since $P = \dfrac{F}{A}$, this results in an increased pressure — 1
    (d) (i) Using a clamp will prevent heat from the student's hand increasing the temperature of the gas in the syringe — 1
    If the temperature of the gas in the syringe is not constant, the experiment would not be valid — 1
    (ii) The suggestion is incorrect because the volume of air in the tubing is not being read from the scale on the syringe — 1
    A longer length of tubing would increase the (systematic) uncertainty in the experiment — 1

9. (a) (i) $3{\cdot}00 \times 10^8\,\text{m s}^{-1}$ — 1
    (ii) $d = vt$ — 1
    $d = 3{\cdot}00 \times 10^8 \times 0{\cdot}0047$ — 1
    $d = 1{\cdot}4 \times 10^6\,\text{m}$ — 1
    (b) $v = f\lambda$ — 1
    $3{\cdot}00 \times 10^8 = 1620 \times 10^6 \times \lambda$ — 1
    $\lambda = 0{\cdot}185\,\text{m}$ — 1
    (c) The waves from the transmitter will diffract over the hill to reach X — 1
    but will not diffract enough to reach Y — 1

10. Demonstrates no understanding — 0 marks
    Demonstrates limited understanding — 1 mark
    Demonstrates reasonable understanding — 2 marks
    Demonstrates good understanding — 3 marks

    This is an open-ended question.

    1 mark: The candidate has demonstrated a limited understanding of the physics involved. The candidate has made some statement(s) which is/are relevant to the situation, showing that at least a little of the physics within the problem is understood.

2 marks: The candidate has demonstrated a reasonable understanding of the physics involved. The candidate makes some statement(s) which is/are relevant to the situation, showing that the problem is understood.

3 marks: Award the maximum available mark to a candidate who has demonstrated a good understanding of the physics involved. The candidate shows a good comprehension of the physics of the situation and has provided a logically correct answer to the question posed. This type of response might include a statement of the principles involved, a relationship or an equation, and the application of these to respond to the problem. This does not mean the answer has to be what might be termed an 'excellent' answer or a 'complete' one.

11. (a) (i) 5800 ± 100 years — 1

    (ii) $26 \rightarrow 13 \rightarrow 6 \cdot 5$
Number of half-lives = 2 — 1
$t = 2 \times 5800$ — 1
$t = 10\,600$ years — 1

    (iii) $\dfrac{125}{25} = 5$ — 1

Activity per 25 g = $\dfrac{40}{5} = 8$ (Bq) — 1

From graph, age = 9700 ± 100 years — 1

(b) The activity (of a sample from the tree) would not have reduced significantly/measurably in 100 years — 1

12. (a) High frequency (or short wavelength) electromagnetic radiation — 1

(b) $D = \dfrac{E}{m}$ — 1

$50 \times 10^{-6} = \dfrac{E}{0 \cdot 10}$ — 1

$E = 5 \cdot 0 \times 10^{-6}$ J — 1

(c) Lead can absorb (some of) the gamma rays — 1

(d) 20 mSv — 1

Acknowledgements

Permission has been sought from all relevant copyright holders and Hodder Gibson is grateful for the use of the following:

Image © Rob Byron/Shutterstock.com (2015 Section 1 page 10);
Image © MarcelClemens/Shutterstock.com (2015 Section 2 page 23);
Image © Procy/Shutterstock.com (2015 Section 2 page 25);
Image © Michael Schneidmiller/Shutterstock.com (2017 Section 2 page 18);
Image © Ljupco Smokovski/Shutterstock.com (2017 Section 2 page 22);
Image © kojihirano/Shutterstock.com (2017 Section 2 page 26);
Image © sandystifler/Shutterstock.com (elements of this image furnished by NASA) (2017 SQP Section 1 page 5);
An extract from 'Dragonfish nebula conceals giant star cluster' by David Shiga, taken from the New Scientist Magazine, 26 January 2011 (www.newscientist.com/blogs/shortsharpscience/2011/01/dragonfish-nebula-conceals-gia.html) © 2011 Reed Business Information — UK. All rights reserved. Distributed by Tribune Media Services (2017 SQP Section 2 page 13);
Image © vadimmmus/Shutterstock.com (2017 SQP Section 2 page 26).